Sarah Flower, a leading nutritionist and author of many cookery books, is passionate about healthy eating and a keen advocate of the sugar-free and low-carb way of eating. She has trained with The Real Meal Revolution, originally set up by Professor Noakes and Jonno Proudfoot, both of whom advise banting/LCHF (low carbohydrate, high fat) and is now herself a banting coach in the UK. Sarah writes for a number of publications, including the *Daily Mail*, *Top Santé* magazine and *Healthista*. She appears regularly on BBC Radio Devon.

Also by Sarah Flower

The Busy Mum's Plan-ahead Cookbook

The Sugar-Free Family Cookbook

Eat Well, Spend Less

The Healthy Lifestyle Diet Cookbook

The Healthy Halogen Cookbook

The Healthy Slow Cooker Cookbook

Perfect Baking with Your Halogen Oven

Halogen Cooking for Two

The Everyday Halogen Family Cookbook

The Everyday Halogen Oven Cookbook

Slow Cook, Fast Food

Low-Carb Slow Cooker

SLOW COOKER
FAMILY CLASSICS

Quick and Easy Recipes the
Whole Family Will Love

Sarah Flower

ROBINSON

ROBINSON

First published in Great Britain in 2019 by Robinson

1 3 5 7 9 10 8 6 4 2

A CIP catalogue record for this book is available from the British Library.

ISBN 978-1-47214-395-2

Designed by Thextension
Typeset in Joanna Nova

Printed and bound in China by C&C Offset Printing Co., Ltd.

Papers used by Robinson are from well-managed forests and responsible sources.

Robinson
An imprint of
Little, Brown Book Group
Carmelite House
50 Victoria Embankment
London EC4Y 0DZ

An Hachette UK Company
www.hachette.co.uk

www.littlebrown.co.uk

The recommendations given in this book are solely intended as education and should not be taken as medical advice.

Contents

Introduction

When I was asked to write a classic family slow cooker cookbook, I jumped at the chance. I wrote my first slow cooker book in 2010. My second slow cooker book, out two years later, was *The Healthy Slow Cooker Cookbook*, and my third slow cooker book, *Low-Carb Slow Cooker*, came out in 2017 and allowed me to explore the low carb, ketogenic way of eating. This book is all about family favourites and traditional recipes. I am not restricting calories, fat or sugar in this book – it is all about real cooking the old-fashioned way.

The ethos of this book is to embrace family favourite recipes and traditional dishes, using cheaper cuts of meat where possible and ensuring every dish is full of flavour. Food is more and more expensive, and families are stretched, not just financially but also for time. Slow cookers really do make our lives so much easier. You can chop all the ingredients in the morning, put them in your slow cooker, turn it on, leave it to cook while you are working or getting on with your busy day, then come home to a nourishing meal. The whole thing requires minimal effort and the result is food that's far, far better for us than any processed ready meal, plus it saves on washing up!

I have a passion for vintage cookbooks and am fascinated by how our tastes have changed over the years. There is a trend now for introducing more traditional, wholesome cuts of meat back into our diet, such as livers and kidneys, both of which are packed with nutrients. I have included dishes using these ingredients in this book, but given the recipes a modern twist. While some traditional meals

ought to stay in the past – braised calf's head, anyone? – there are plenty of classic dishes that are as delicious and wholesome as ever.

In recent years, many of us have moved towards eating more plant-based meals. While these aren't quite so classic or traditional, I have included a vegan and vegetarian chapter so that your slow cooker can cater for any dietary requirement. Also, check out the soup recipes as I've included a number of vegan and vegetarian options there.

You may be wondering why I've included an entire chapter on Christmas. This is the time of year when the slow cooker comes into its own. When we are all busy running around in a bubble of festive stress, the slow cooker can reliably cook a meal, leaving us to get on with our Christmas chores.

The dessert chapter, one of my favourites, is full of classic family recipes, some of which you may recognise from your childhood. I have not tweaked these to make them healthier, but if you read the opening paragraphs of the dessert chapter, you will find my top tips on how to adapt these recipes for your specific dietary requirements – for sugar-free, vegan and gluten-free diets.

One thing I really want to stress: please read the technical first chapter, especially if you are new to the slow cooker. It is really important to get to know your slow cooker as they can vary. Older slow cookers or very basic ones can often cook a little hotter than they should. If your slow cooker is bubbling away and liquid is evaporating, it may be best to cook on the Low setting rather than High and opt for the lower end of the timings – you also need to ensure your slow cooker does not overheat.

If you haven't used a slow cooker before, buy a multi-cooker that switches from a sauté/hob facility to slow cooker as this does make life so much easier. Also, ensure it has a timer that switches to warm once the cooking time is reached. This is really important if you are coming home late – you don't want to come home to a bowl of mush instead of your lovely casserole. If you don't have an Auto timing function, you may want to consider using a timing plug, especially if you are out all day and can't monitor your slow cooker. This will at least ensure it only cooks for the suggested times. You need the slow cooker lid to form a good seal and prevent evaporation. The temperatures and timings listed in the recipes are only guidelines. The idea is slow, low and long.

I do hope you enjoy this book. If you do, maybe you would like to get in touch. It is always lovely to hear from readers. You can contact me by visiting my website at www.sarahflower.co.uk, or on Twitter and Instagram @ MsSarahFlower. I will also be sharing recipes and cookery videos on my Facebook pages – HealthySlowCooker and EverydaySugarFree.

I hope you enjoy the recipes and the delicious meals you are about to create!

Sarah x

How to use your slow cooker

Slow cookers gained popularity in the 1970s, but the principle of slow cooking goes back hundreds of years – consider those large stock pots seen dangling from kitchen ranges! The slow cooker revolutionised meal preparation, enabling the creation of wholesome meals ready for your return after a busy day. It was incredibly popular, but sadly became relegated to kitchen cupboards as we moved into the Thatcher years of 'loadsamoney', when frugal cooking went out of fashion. Cheaper cuts of meats fell out of favour and there seemed to be no real reason to keep the slow cooker in our kitchens – the microwave and processed food became the homemaker's choice for a busy lifestyle, and the poor slow cooker was forgotten. Thankfully, we are now seeing a revival as people come to realise that these clever machines can not only save us time, but also ensure that minimal nutrients are lost in the cooking process.

You can buy a slow cooker from as little as £15, and multi-cookers, of which I am a huge fan, are becoming increasingly popular. When purchasing a slow cooker or multi-cooker, it is important to consider how it is going to be used. Think about the size of the machine: some look quite big but the actual size of the stock pot may not be sufficient. If you are cooking for a large family or like to plan ahead and freeze food, you may be better off spending more money and investing in a larger machine. Go to an electrical store where you can actually view the machines; even if you end up buying your machine online instead of in a store, it will give you an idea of the machines on sale and what your requirements are.

I would also strongly recommend buying the best you can afford. These are the functions I absolutely love:

MULTI-FUNCTION This basically means you can switch from sauté to slow cooking all in one machine. This saves on time and washing up, which is a 'win win' for me.

TIMER I feel this feature is absolutely vital. My machine allows me to set a cooking time on the High or Low temperature settings. Once that time has been reached, the machine automatically switches to Warm, ensuring my food does not spoil.

AUTO Some machines have an Auto function. This means it will start off cooking on High and once the temperature has been reached it will switch to Low. It then remains on Low for the duration of the set cooking time.

If you have an older-style slow cooker, where the heating element is directly beneath the inner pot, the heat is less evenly distributed, which can cause hot spots and potentially burn a dish. With baking recipes, if you have an older machine, it's worth using a trivet, wire rack, balls of foil or an upturned saucer in the base of the slow cooker to raise your dish from the heat source and ensure it cooks evenly. Trivets aren't required when using newer machines and multi-cookers, as the heat is more evenly distributed.

Know your machine

THIS IS REALLY IMPORTANT! Every machine is different. If you are buying a new machine, buy one with a timing switch so it can turn itself to Warm once the cooking time is reached – this saves any potential disasters with overcooking. Newer machines often have an automatic switch that turns the cooking setting to High until temperature is reached then switches to Low. Most have a High and Low setting.

If you have an old machine, check its temperature gauge is working correctly. The Low setting on a slow cooker is approximately 95°C and High is 130–150°C. You can check this with a thermometer. Some can get much hotter, which can result in your food burning on the base or around the edges when left on High for long periods. It may also evaporate liquid faster so you may need to use more stock. If you are concerned that it might get too hot, only use it on Low. The temperature should not create a boil; it should be a low, slow cook and not a fast, boiling cook.

Multi-cookers

I am a massive fan of the slow cooker and thought I knew all there is to know about these machines. That was until I discovered the multi-cooker. Initially I thought it was a bit of a gimmick – it can steam, slow cook, roast, sauté and bake – but it has won me over. I have tested several of these machines, but the Crock-pot Multi-cooker has now taken pride of place on my kitchen worktop.

Some slow cookers have a sauté option, which can be a bit hit and miss, but the multi-cooker really is an all-in-one cooking experience. The sauté option allows you to sauté with five different temperature settings. The slow cooker function allows you to choose from High, Low and Warm. Once the cooking time has been reached, it automatically switches to Warm mode – perfect if you are late home for dinner! The roasting rack can be used either on the Low or High setting, depending on the size of your joint. If I'm cooking a small joint of beef, I brown it first with the sauté function, then add some vegetables to the base, pop my beef joint on top and switch to Roast for 45 minutes. It cooks perfectly, and the vegetables and juices at the base make a delicious stock. While the beef is resting, I wash out the slow cooker bowl, add some water to the base and steam my vegetables in 7 minutes. So easy. My multi-cooker also has a bake function.

To sauté or not to sauté

Slow cooker recipes often suggest you sauté onions or brown meat before cooking the rest of the dish. I have tried with and without, and to be honest I really did not notice much difference in the taste, but sautéing does help to seal the meat and the colour is certainly much more appealing. If you are cooking a whole chicken, for example, remember that it will not brown, so may look a bit unappealing. Sautéing the chicken also stops it from flaking into the dish. Coating meat with flour can also help if you want a thicker sauce. Remember the slow cooker is designed not to evaporate much liquid, so you may find you need to thicken the dish until you get used to the way your machine works – they are all different! All multi-cookers offer a sauté option. You may find that your slow cooker also has a sauté function; others come with hob-proof dishes, allowing you to transfer the slow cooker pot from one heat source to another. Refer to the manufacturer's instructions for more information.

Slow cooking tips

All slow cookers come with detailed manufacturer's instructions, recipe suggestions and even a useful helpline to call if you get stuck. I strongly advise reading these booklets before using your machine. Here are some reminders:

1 Preheat your slow cooker, following the manufacturer's instructions.

2 As a rule of thumb, 1 hour in a conventional oven equates to 2–3 hours on High in a slow cooker, or 6 hours on Low setting. Some slow cookers have an Auto setting – this essentially means it heats up quickly on High, then when it reaches temperature, reverts to Low for the remaining cooking time. This helps food, especially meat, reach a safe temperature quickly. Some machines have a Warm setting, which is useful if the food has reached its maximum cooking time and you are just wanting to keep it warm, but, really, the Low setting is sufficient and most food can cook for 10 hours without starting to spoil.

3 You may need to adjust the liquid content of your dish depending on your personal taste but remember you do need liquid to cook the food. All food must be submerged in liquid before cooking – potatoes especially may bob around on top and go black, so push them into the stock. The manufacturer's guidelines should detail the minimum and maximum fill levels for your machine. Less liquid evaporates when you use a slow cooker so you may need to thicken soups or casseroles towards the end of the cooking time. Adding more water or stock is simple and can be done at any stage. If you find liquid is quickly evaporating, the slow cooker may be on too high a setting.

4 The key point to remember is that once you set your slow cooker to begin cooking, you shouldn't keep removing the lid as this reduces the temperature and means it will take longer for the slow cooker to get back up to the required temperature. The outer edge of the lid forms a seal. Sometimes this may spit or bubble, but this is quite normal. Only remove it when absolutely necessary, ideally just when it finishes cooking or, if necessary, in the last 30 minutes of cooking, to add key ingredients. If you are the sort of person who likes to keep an eye on things, opt for a slow cooker with a glass lid (though this is not foolproof as they do get steamed up!).

5 Always defrost any frozen ingredients thoroughly before placing them in the slow cooker, especially meat. The slow cooker is designed to cook safely at low temperatures; however, if your cooker does not maintain the required heat, it could increase the risk of food poisoning caused by the spread of bacteria. Frozen foods such as peas, sweetcorn, other quick-cook vegetables, and prawns, should only be added in the last 30 minutes of cooking time.

6 When adding liquids such as stock or water, to maintain the temperature, it is better to use warm liquids (not boiling) rather than cold.

7 Pasta should only be added in the last 30 minutes of cooking time as it goes very soggy and breaks up during longer cooking times.

8 Fresh herbs can be used, but tend to lose their flavour over longer cooking times. If you are using fresh herbs, add them in the last 30 minutes of cooking time.

9 Vegetables, especially root vegetables, take much longer to cook than meat. You can speed up the process by sautéing the vegetables before adding them to the dish, or simply cutting them into smaller chunks. Make sure the vegetables are thoroughly immersed in the stock, ideally on the base as this is the hottest area.

Cakes

I have made cakes in the slow cooker and they have been really tasty, though they have a different texture from oven-baked cakes. Cakes that respond well to being slow cooked include fruit cakes, sponge puddings and Christmas pudding. I simply place the cake dish in the slow cooker and add water to the base to create a bain-marie.

Freezing

If you want to get ahead, why not double up a recipe and freeze extra portions? To do this, make sure you remove the dish from the slow cooker and allow it to chill thoroughly before freezing. You can buy special freezer bags for liquid-based meals such as soups or casseroles. Make sure they have completely defrosted before reheating.

Conversion charts and symbols

Weight

METRIC	IMPERIAL
25g	1oz
50g	2oz
75g	3oz
100g	4oz
150g	5oz
175g	6oz
200g	7oz
225g	8oz
250g	9oz
300g	10oz
350g	12oz
400g	14oz
450g	1lb

Measurements

METRIC	IMPERIAL
5cm	2in
10cm	4in
13cm	5in
15cm	6in
18cm	7in
20cm	8in
25cm	10in
30cm	12in

Liquids

METRIC	IMPERIAL	US CUP
5ml	1 tsp	1 tsp
15ml	1 tbsp	1 tbsp
50ml	2fl oz	3 tbsp
60ml	2½fl oz	¼ cup
75ml	3fl oz	⅓ cup
100ml	4fl oz	scant ½ cup
125ml	4½ oz	½ cup
150ml	5fl oz	⅔ cup
200ml	7fl oz	scant 1 cup
250ml	9fl oz	1 cup
300ml	½ pint	1¼ cups
350ml	12fl oz	1⅓ cups
400ml	¾ pint	1¾ cups
500ml	17fl oz	2 cups
600ml	1 pt	2½ cups

❄ Can be frozen

Ⓥ Suitable for vegetarians

VG Suitable for vegans

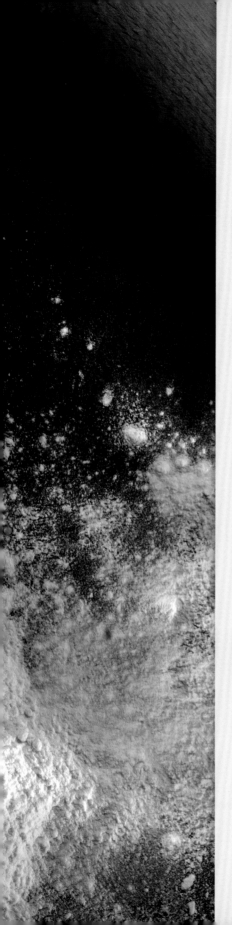

Breakfast

We don't often think of using the slow cooker to make breakfast, but it really can be useful, especially if your machine has a timer function (don't worry if your machine doesn't have this function – you can use a timer on your slow cooker plug). You can make porridge, granola, yogurt and even a cooked breakfast in your slow cooker, all of which are very nice to wake up to in the morning and require very little effort. Don't forget to look in the Pantry chapter (page 194) where you will find some delicious jams and curds, ideal to have with your slow-cooked natural yogurt or add to your breakfast toast.

For a slow-cooker full English breakfast, place the beans, sausages and mushrooms with butter in individual ovenproof pots ready to slow cook for breakfast – genius!

This is a lovely way to start the day when served with some homemade natural yogurt (see page 16) or with porridge. Once cooked, it will keep well in an airtight container in the fridge for up to 48 hours.

Winter Fruit Compote

SERVES 4

NUTRITIONAL INFORMATION
PER SERVING
158 Kcals
0.5g fat
33g net carbohydrates
6g fibre
2g protein

INGREDIENTS
75g dried prunes
75g dried figs
75g dried apricots
50g raisins or sultanas
30g dried apple rings, diced
400g tin sliced pears, diced,
  with juice
1 tsp ground cinnamon
1 tsp ground allspice
2 oranges, peeled and sliced,
  plus grated zest and juice
  of 1 orange
1 banana
honey, to taste (optional)

1 Preheat your slow cooker, following the manufacturer's instructions.

2 Place the dried fruit in the slow cooker with all the remaining ingredients apart from the banana. Add 150ml water.

3 Set to Low, cover and cook for 4 hours.

4 Just before serving, slice the banana, remove the lid of the slow cooker and add the banana. Stir well and serve immediately, including all the delicious juice. If you prefer a sweeter juice, add honey to taste.

While this appears in the breakfast chapter, really it's suitable for any meal. It is perfect for using up leftover vegetables and the recipe can be very easily adapted to suit a variety of flavour combinations. The recipe below uses spinach and Brussels sprouts, but you can use any vegetable you wish. Alternatively, for a very simple recipe, just use onion, rice, haddock and eggs along with the herbs and spices.

Loaded Smoked Haddock Kedgeree

SERVES 4

NUTRITIONAL INFORMATION
PER SERVING
451 Kcals
12g fat
47g net carbohydrates
6.5g fibre
35g protein

INGREDIENTS
1 onion, finely chopped
200g brown long-grain rice
50g red lentils, rinsed
1–2 red or green chillies, finely
  chopped (optional)
800ml hot chicken or fish
  stock
1 bay leaf
1 tsp ground turmeric
½ tsp ground cardamom
1 heaped tsp mild curry
  powder
1 cinnamon stick
1 tbsp butter, plus extra
  for greasing
300g smoked haddock pieces
8 Brussels sprouts, halved
50g baby leaf spinach
4 eggs
salt and ground black pepper

1 Grease the base of your stock pot with butter.

2 Preheat your slow cooker, following the manufacturer's instructions.

3 Rinse the rice well until the water runs clear (this will ensure the excess starch is removed).

4 Place all the ingredients in the slow cooker apart from the butter, haddock, Brussels sprouts, spinach and eggs. Stir well and season with salt and pepper.

5 Set to High, cover and cook for 1½–2½ hours, or set to Low and cook for 5–6 hours, until the rice is evenly cooked. If you can, check the rice occasionally, give a stir and ensure it is cooking evenly. If you need to leave the slow cooker unattended, cook on Low.

6 Remove the lid and stir well to fluff up the rice. Stir in the butter, haddock, Brussels sprouts and spinach.

7 Cover and cook on High for another 30 minutes. You may need to add a little more stock if it has all been absorbed. Please watch this as it can burn if your slow cooker has a tendency to overheat – if this is the case, cook on Low instead of High. You may need to increase the cooking time by 15 minutes if you do this.

8 Boil the eggs for 7–10 minutes, depending on how you prefer the yolk. Pop in cold water immediately after cooking. Peel and quarter the eggs.

9 Serve the rice topped with the eggs.

I love full-fat yogurt, but it is becoming more and more difficult to get this in the supermarket, with the misconception that low fat is healthiest. Full-fat yogurt is rich and thick, packed with protein and is very good for you. I make this deliciously creamy yogurt using full-fat milk and have even made it with cream for a decadent treat. You can buy starter kits for yogurt-making, but they are expensive and unnecessary – just use some live plain yogurt to start you off. You don't need to add any sweetener. I serve it with fresh figs, berries and my favourite homemade granola (see page 20).

Thick and Creamy Yogurt

MAKES 1 LITRE

NUTRITIONAL
INFORMATION PER 100G
151 Kcals
13.5g fat
4.1g net carbohydrates
3.4g protein

EQUIPMENT
You will need a thermometer, a sheet of muslin and a colander.

INGREDIENTS
1 litre full-fat milk
250ml double cream
5 tbsp live plain yogurt

1 Preheat your slow cooker, following the manufacturer's instructions.

2 Pour the milk and cream into the slow cooker and stir to combine well. Set the slow cooker to High.

3 You need the mixture to reach 80–85°C, so you will need a thermometer to check this. Once this temperature is reached, turn off the slow cooker but keep the lid on and let it cool until it reaches 40–45°C.

4 When it has cooled to temperature, transfer a ladleful of the mixture into a bowl and stir in the yogurt. Pour this very gently around the rest of the mixture in the slow cooker: do not mix, but ensure it is evenly drizzled over the mixture. Pop the lid back on immediately to ensure the temperature remains constant. You can wrap your slow cooker in a thick towel or similar, especially if it is in a drafty kitchen or has an ill-fitting lid, to maintain the temperature – you need to ensure it stays warm. Leave overnight (10–12 hours).

5 The next day, the yogurt may resemble cottage cheese. You will need to drain off the whey. I use a sheet of muslin to line a colander, then tip in the yogurt and leave it to drain naturally for 15–30 minutes before gently squeezing out the excess liquid, leaving me with a thick yogurt.

6 Store the yogurt in the fridge in an airtight container for up to a week. You can use some of this yogurt to start another batch.

It is good to wake up to your breakfast with little effort. This is a basic porridge recipe, but you can add your own flavourings to the oats, for example chopped dates, chopped apple, grated carrot or dried fruit all work well. If your slow cooker does not have a timer function, you can use a timing plug. Serve with fresh fruit or with the Winter Fruit Compote on page 12.

Overnight Slow-cooked Porridge

SERVES 4

NUTRITIONAL INFORMATION
PER SERVING
203 Kcals
7g fat
26g net carbohydrates
2.4g fibre
7.8g protein

EQUIPMENT
You will need a ceramic or ovenproof bowl and foil.

INGREDIENTS
125g wholegrain jumbo oats
500ml full-fat milk, plus extra
  to serve
1 tsp ground cinnamon
  (optional)

1 Preheat your slow cooker, following the manufacturer's instructions.

2 Combine the oats, milk and cinnamon (if using) with 400ml water and place in a ceramic or ovenproof bowl. Add a heatproof lid. If you don't have a lid, make one with foil and secure well to seal.

3 Place the bowl in the slow cooker (on top of a trivet if necessary, see page 3), set to Low and cook for 6–8 hours.

4 When ready to serve, remove the lid, stir well and add more milk until you get the desired consistency. Sweeten to taste before serving.

This nutty, fruity granola has a gentle cinnamon and honey flavour. I love serving this with natural Greek yogurt.

Fruity Granola

MAKES ABOUT 40 SERVINGS
(V)

NUTRITIONAL INFORMATION
PER 30G SERVING
165 Kcals
10g fat
14g net carbohydrates
2.8g fibre
3.3g protein

INGREDIENTS
250g mixed nuts (brazil,
  hazelnuts, almonds,
  macadamias, walnuts)
100g pecan nuts
400g wholegrain jumbo oats
100g wheat flakes
75g flaked almonds
100g coconut flakes
50g coconut oil
2 tsp ground cinnamon
4 tbsp honey (or to taste)
75g sultanas
75g raisins
75g dried cranberries
50g dried apricots, diced
50g dried apple slices, diced

1 Preheat your slow cooker, following the manufacturer's instructions.

2 Place the nuts in a freezer bag and bash them with a rolling pin until they are in small pieces. I prefer breaking them into pieces like this as it's a good stress-reliever but also because a food processor tends to over-process them and if you are not careful you can end up with nutty dust!

3 Place the crushed nuts in a bowl and add the oats, wheat flakes, flaked almonds and coconut flakes.

4 Melt the coconut oil in a jug, then add the cinnamon and honey and combine well.

5 Pour the coconut oil mixture over the granola mix and stir well until the oil coats all the nuts.

6 Pour the mixture into the slow cooker, set to High, cover and cook for 1½–2 hours, stirring occasionally.

7 Remove from the slow cooker and allow to cool before adding the dried fruit. Combine well. Store in an airtight container for 3–4 weeks.

NOTE
Slow cookers can vary in temperature. If you think your slow cooker tends to get too hot, cook this on the Low setting to avoid burning.

One for the kids or the chocoholic! You can monitor the sugar content as this is made without sweetener, which can be added once cooked.

Overnight Chocolate Porridge

SERVES 4

NUTRITIONAL INFORMATION
PER SERVING
220 Kcals
8.1g fat
26g net carbohydrates
3g fibre
9g protein

EQUIPMENT
You will need a ceramic or
ovenproof bowl and foil.

INGREDIENTS
125g wholegrain jumbo oats
500ml full-fat milk
1 tsp vanilla bean paste
2–3 heaped tsp cocoa powder

1 Preheat your slow cooker, following the manufacturer's instructions.

2 Combine the oats, milk, 500ml water, vanilla and cocoa powder and place in a ceramic or ovenproof bowl. Add a heatproof lid. If you don't have a lid, make one with foil and secure well to seal.

3 Place the bowl in the slow cooker, set to Low and cook for 6–8 hours.

4 When ready to serve, remove the lid, stir well and add more milk until you get the desired consistency. Sweeten to taste before serving.

NOTE
Why not serve with sliced banana and sliced almonds or a spoonful of almond butter?

Soups

Soups are bursting with nutrients.
Quick and easy, they can be served as a snack or a
nutritious meal. Soups are a great way of getting
extra vegetables into your family's diet. They are
also cheap to make and very filling. Best of all, as
they are slow cooked at a low temperature, the
nutrients are maintained, making the soup ultra-
healthy. If you or your child has a packed lunch,
why not invest in a small flask and fill it with your
homemade soup – a perfect way to fill up and
warm the body, especially during the winter
months. Most soups can be frozen, so fill your
freezer with individual portions ready for lunches.

Soup-making advice

Which stock?

Stock cubes can be quite overpowering and high in salt and sugar, but there are some great products available now that give soups a more natural flavour. I make my own stock but if I am in a hurry or want a burst of stock flavour, I use gel stock pots. Try to make your own stock as it is packed with nutrients, particularly if you use animal bones; I am a huge fan of bone stock (see recipes in the Pantry chapter). You can freeze stock, so make big batches.

Puréeing soup

Some people like a chunky soup, others like a smooth soup. When puréeing a soup, I use an electric hand-held blender (some call it a stick blender). It is simple to use and saves you having to wash up another piece of equipment when transferring to a liquidiser or blender. Make sure the end of the stick blender is fully submerged in the soup or you will end up with soup everywhere! For a fine-textured soup, pass it through a sieve.

Chunky soup

To thicken a chunky soup, simply remove about a quarter of the soup and purée it, then add it back to the soup.

Liquid: thick or thin?

Liquid doesn't evaporate in the slow cooker as much as it does with other cooking methods, so you may need to thicken slow-cooker soups. To do this, mix 2–3 teaspoons of cornflour with 50ml of water. Stir this thickening mixture into the soup in the slow cooker, ensuring it is evenly mixed, turn the setting to High and cook for 15–30 minutes until thick. Alternatively, remove some of the chunky soup and purée it (see above). Adding more water or stock to loosen the soup is simple and can be done at any stage.

Pulses and beans

Adding pulses and beans is a cheap way to bulk out a soup (or any meal). It also adds essential nutrients and can keep you feeling fuller for longer.

Adding dairy

Cream, milk, Greek yogurt and crème fraîche can sometimes separate when cooked in a slow cooker for long periods, so it's best to add them just before serving.

Chanterelle mushrooms are a type of wild mushroom with a lovely mellow flavour. I like combining them with chestnut mushrooms. If you can't get chanterelle mushrooms, use mushrooms of your choice, though I would urge you to add a mix of varieties to this soup. Most supermarkets sell a variety pack, containing shiitake, oyster, enoki, maitake etc., which will all work well.

Creamy Chanterelle Mushroom Soup

SERVES 4

❄ Ⓥ

NUTRITIONAL INFORMATION PER SERVING
502 Kcals
41g fat
22g net carbohydrates
4.7g fibre
8.1g protein

INGREDIENTS
30g dried porcini mushrooms
400g chanterelle mushrooms, halved if large
200g oyster or shiitake mushrooms, chopped
100g chestnut mushrooms, halved
1 onion, finely chopped
2 garlic cloves, finely chopped
2 tbsp dry sherry
200ml hot vegetable or chicken stock
1 tsp thyme
½ tsp tarragon
300ml double cream
juice of ½ lemon
1 tbsp cornflour (optional)
salt and ground black pepper
fresh tarragon or thyme, to serve (optional)

1 Preheat your slow cooker, following the manufacturer's instructions.

2 Soak the porcini mushrooms in a bowl of just-boiled water until rehydrated. This takes about 10–15 minutes. Once hydrated, add them to the slow cooker, along with the soaking liquid. Set aside a few chanterelles to garnish.

3 Combine all the ingredients in the slow cooker, apart from the double cream, lemon juice and cornflour. Mix well, season with salt and pepper, set the slow cooker to Low, cover and cook for 4 hours.

4 Remove the lid and use a stick blender to whizz the soup until smooth. Add the cream and the lemon juice and combine well. Taste and season again if needed.

5 If you want to thicken the soup, mix the cornflour with a little water to form a paste, stir into the soup and combine well. Cover and cook on High for 30 minutes.

6 Serve with a garnish of sautéed chanterelle mushrooms or fresh tarragon or thyme leaves.

This thick, slightly spicy soup is very filling. It's nice in the autumn when pumpkins are so readily available, but you can of course use any squash you prefer in this recipe – it works well with butternut squash. Sprinkle with toasted pumpkin seeds for extra nutrition and crunch.

Spiced Pumpkin and Carrot Soup

SERVES 4

NUTRITIONAL INFORMATION
PER SERVING
81 Kcals
1.7g fat
11g net carbohydrates
3.1g fibre
4.3g protein

INGREDIENTS
1 onion, diced
3 carrots, diced
1 small pumpkin (500–700g),
  peeled, deseeded and diced
2 garlic cloves, crushed
3cm piece of fresh ginger,
  peeled and roughly chopped
1 tbsp coriander seeds, crushed
1 tsp ground coriander
½ tsp ground cumin
1 tsp thyme
1 tsp sumac
450ml hot vegetable, chicken
  or bone stock
salt and ground black pepper
cream or yogurt, to serve

1 Preheat your slow cooker, following the manufacturer's instructions.

2 Place all the vegetables in the slow cooker. Add the herbs and spices, cover with the hot stock, and season with salt and pepper.

3 Set to Low, cover and cook for 6–8 hours.

4 When ready to serve, remove the lid and use a stick blender to whizz the soup until smooth. Taste and season again if necessary.

5 Serve the soup in bowls and add a whirl of single cream or yogurt to each serving.

White asparagus is in season from mid-May, but if you can't find white asparagus, you can of course use green. This is a lovely soup for a dinner party starter. If you prefer, remove a few pieces of cooked asparagus blending the soup, then add them with the crème fraîche mixture. Serve it with some rustic homemade bread.

White Asparagus Soup

SERVES 4

NUTRITIONAL INFORMATION
PER SERVING
213 Kcals
13g fat
8.6g net carbohydrates
3.4g fibre
7.8g protein

INGREDIENTS
500g white asparagus,
   trimmed and chopped
1 onion, finely chopped
150ml hot vegetable or
   chicken stock
150ml white wine
3 egg yolks
200g crème fraîche
salt and ground black pepper
2 tbsp chopped fresh parsley,
   plus extra to garnish

1 Preheat your slow cooker, following the manufacturer's instructions.

2 Place the asparagus and onion in the slow cooker. Add the stock and the wine and season well with black pepper.

3 Set to High, cover and cook for 1½–2 hours.

4 Remove the lid and use a stick blender to whizz the soup until smooth.

5 Beat the egg yolks and crème fraîche together in a bowl. Season to taste.

6 Add the crème fraîche mixture to the soup, stirring quickly to ensure the mix is dispersed but does not go lumpy.

7 Cover and cook for another 15 minutes on High before serving. Garnish with parsley.

This soup originates from Georgia. It's a really tasty beef soup – it's almost a stew, so ensure you chop everything small! This is my version which is very popular in our house, especially in the winter months when we want a nourishing and warming lunch.

Beef Kharcho Soup

SERVES 6

NUTRITIONAL INFORMATION
PER SERVING
281 Kcals
11g fat
22g net carbohydrates
4.4g fibre
19g Protein

INGREDIENTS
2 tsp olive oil or coconut oil
300g stewing beef, diced
1 onion, finely diced
1 red pepper, deseeded and
  finely diced
1–2 red or green chillies,
  sliced (to taste)
2 garlic cloves, crushed
1 celery stick, finely diced
1 carrot, finely diced
400g tin chopped tomatoes
2 tbsp tomato purée
500–650ml hot bone or
  beef stock
2 tsp sweet paprika
2 tsp ground coriander
2 tsp dried mint
½ tsp fenugreek seeds
100g basmati rice, rinsed
salt and ground black pepper
a small handful of fresh
  coriander leaves, chopped,
  to serve
50g walnuts, toasted and
  crushed, to serve

1 Preheat your slow cooker, following the manufacturer's instructions.

2 If your slow cooker has a sauté function, you can use this; if not, use a sauté pan on your hob. Heat the olive oil or coconut oil, add the beef and cook until brown. Place in the slow cooker (if you used a separate pan).

3 Add the remaining ingredients to the slow cooker, except the fresh coriander leaves and crushed walnuts. Season with salt and pepper.

4 Set to Low, cover and cook for 7–8 hours.

5 When ready to serve, garnish with the chopped coriander and the walnuts.

This is a very chunky, filling version of minestrone soup. Feel free to use whatever pasta shapes you prefer. A sprinkling of grated Parmesan over each serving is delicious.

Chunky Minestrone Soup

SERVES 6

NUTRITIONAL INFORMATION
PER SERVING
172 Kcals
2.7g fat
24g net carbohydrates
5.7g fibre
9.4g protein

INGREDIENTS
1 onion, finely chopped
2 garlic cloves, crushed
1 red pepper, deseeded and
  diced
1 large carrot, diced or sliced
1 sweet potato, peeled and
  diced
1 courgette, sliced
1 celery stick, diced
500ml hot bone, vegetable
  or chicken stock
2 tbsp tomato purée
1 bay leaf
1 tsp paprika
2 tsp oregano
1 tsp parsley
75g dried small pasta
  (such as ditalini, orzo
  or spirali)
75g frozen edamame
  (soya) beans
salt and ground black pepper
fresh basil leaves, to serve

1 Preheat your slow cooker, following the manufacturer's instructions.

2 Add all ingredients apart from the pasta and the edamame beans to the slow cooker. Make sure the stock is hot as this will help maintain the right temperature.

3 Set to Low, cover and cook for 6–8 hours.

4 Remove the lid, add the pasta and edamame beans, and more stock if needed, replace the lid and cook at High for another 30 minutes.

5 Serve garnished with fresh basil.

This is a very healthy soup, with a vibrant red colour. Adding some warming spices lifts this soup to another level. Serve with a swirl of natural yogurt or crème fraîche, some mint leaves and a handful of toasted seeds.

Beetroot and Apple Soup

SERVES 4–6

 VG

NUTRITIONAL INFORMATION PER SERVING (FOR 6 SERVINGS)
165 Kcals
2g fat
27g net carbohydrates
5.3g fibre
6.6g protein

INGREDIENTS
500g beetroot, peeled and diced
3 apples, peeled and diced
1 red onion, diced
3cm piece of fresh ginger, peeled and finely chopped
1 tsp ground coriander
½ tsp ground cinnamon
1 tsp caraway seeds
500ml hot bone, chicken or vegetable stock
grated zest and juice of 1 lime
salt and ground black pepper

1 Ensure you cut the beetroot and apples into same-sized pieces so they cook evenly.

2 Preheat your slow cooker, following the manufacturer's instructions.

3 Put all the ingredients in the slow cooker. Make sure the stock is hot when adding as this will help maintain the right temperature.

4 Set to Low, cover and cook for 6–8 hours, or if you want a faster meal, set to High and cook for 3–4 hours.

5 Remove the lid and use a stick blender to whizz the soup until smooth (or transfer it to a liquidiser to blend), adding more stock if needed. Season to taste with salt and pepper and serve.

I love the rich flavour of this soup, and it's wonderfully creamy and very filling, too. You can also garnish with walnuts and cashews. If you are not a fan of garlic, leave it out.

Cauliflower, Garlic and Blue Cheese Soup

SERVES 4–6

NUTRITIONAL INFORMATION
PER SERVING
(FOR 6 SERVINGS)
361 Kcals
19g fat
26g net carbohydrates
5g fibre
20g protein

INGREDIENTS
1 onion, finely chopped
3 garlic cloves, finely chopped
1 celery stick, finely chopped
1 potato, peeled and finely
  chopped
750g cauliflower, roughly
  chopped
450ml hot bone, vegetable or
  chicken stock
200g Stilton or other blue
  cheese, plus extra to serve
salt and ground black pepper
chopped fresh parsley leaves,
  to serve

1 Preheat your slow cooker, following the manufacturer's instructions.

2 Place all the ingredients, except the cheese, in the slow cooker.

3 Set to Low, cover and cook for 5½ hours.

4 Remove the lid, crumble in the 200g blue cheese and stir well. Set to High, cover and cook for 30 minutes.

5 Use a stick blender to whizz the soup until smooth, and season to taste.

6 Garnish with some crumbled cheese and chopped fresh parsley.

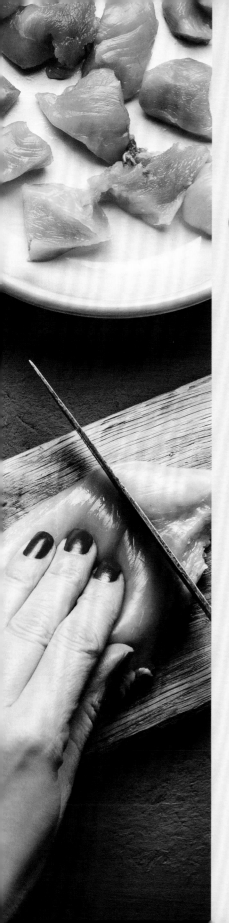

Chicken

Chicken is one of the most popular
meats in the UK. It works well in the slow cooker
but does not need the lengthy slow-cook that
tougher cuts of meat need (such as lamb or beef).

Most families opt for chicken breast but
consider using thighs and leg meat instead as
these are much tastier and often cheaper. You
can buy them skinless and boneless if you prefer.
You can also swap chicken for turkey, which is
higher in protein.

Don't forget to save your bones if you are
cooking a roast chicken. They make an excellent
and very nourishing chicken stock – see the Pantry
chapter (page 200) for the recipe.

I adore Italian flavours and this dish, a delicious mix of tomatoes, herbs, cannellini beans and chicken, is no exception. Cannellini beans are a good source of protein and are also economical, so great for bulking out a dish. This is simple but utterly scrumptious. Serve it with crusty bread and salad.

Italian Chicken and Bean Casserole

SERVES 4

NUTRITIONAL INFORMATION
PER SERVING
438 Kcals
19g fat
20g net carbohydrates
6.7g fibre
43g protein

INGREDIENTS
2 tsp olive oil or coconut oil
1kg pieces chicken (thigh, leg
  or breast)
100g diced smoked pancetta
400g tin whole cherry
  tomatoes
2 red peppers, deseeded and
  roughly chopped
2 tbsp sun-dried tomato paste
2 tsp oregano
1 tsp basil
1 tsp thyme
400g tin cannellini beans,
  drained
250ml hot chicken stock
salt and ground black pepper
fresh basil leaves, to garnish

1 Preheat your slow cooker, following the manufacturer's instructions.

2 If your slow cooker has a sauté option, you can use this; if not, use a sauté pan on your hob. Heat the olive oil or coconut oil. Add the chicken and pancetta and cook for 2–3 minutes to brown the meat. Place the meat in the slow cooker (if you used a separate pan).

3 Add all the remaining ingredients to the slow cooker except the fresh basil leaves.

4 Set to Low, cover and cook for 6–8 hours.

5 Garnish with basil leaves and serve.

Fajitas isn't a dish you would normally associate with the slow cooker but it is so useful when you want to come home to a family-friendly dish your kids will love. Serve the chicken in tortilla wraps with some salad leaves, guacamole and a dollop of sour cream.

Chicken Fajitas

SERVES 4

NUTRITIONAL
INFORMATION PER SERVING
(WITHOUT WRAPS)
214 Kcals
1.9g fat
15g net carbohydrates
4.1g fibre
32g protein

INGREDIENTS
1 large onion, sliced
3 peppers (any colour),
  deseeded and sliced
500g chicken breast, cut into
  thick strips
100ml hot chicken stock
salt and ground black pepper

FOR THE FAJITA SEASONING
1–2 tsp chilli powder
  (I use mild)
½ tsp garlic powder
2 tsp paprika
1 tsp oregano
½ tsp ground cumin
1 tsp onion powder
1 tsp parsley
2 tsp chicken seasoning

1 Preheat your slow cooker, following the manufacturer's instructions.

2 Combine the fajita seasoning ingredients in a bowl.

3 Place the onion, peppers and chicken in the slow cooker. Add the fajita seasoning and stir well until the chicken and vegetables are coated. Season with salt and pepper and add the chicken stock.

4 Set to Low, cover and cook for 6 hours.

5 When ready to serve, place the mixture (drained of any excess liquid, if necessary) in a bowl. Serve in wraps with salad leaves, guacamole and sour cream.

TOP TIP
Scale up the fajita seasoning and store in a jar ready to use for another dish.

This is quite a hot dish, so adjust the spices to suit your own taste. If you double up the recipe, you can freeze what you don't use, ready for another meal. You can use chicken breasts, legs or thighs for this dish – thighs are the most economical and the tastiest, in my opinion. Serve with basmati or cauliflower rice and naan bread for a great family curry night.

Chicken Vindaloo

SERVES 4

NUTRITIONAL INFORMATION PER SERVING
260 Kcals
12.4g fat
5.7g net carbohydrates
1.9g fibre
30.9g protein

INGREDIENTS
600g boneless chicken, diced
  (breast, leg or thigh)
1 large red onion, diced
250ml hot bone stock or
  chicken stock
salt and ground black pepper

FOR THE CURRY PASTE
2 tbsp olive oil
1 red or green chilli
2 garlic cloves
2–4 tbsp vindaloo curry paste
  (to taste)
1 tsp ground turmeric
1 tsp ground cumin
3 tomatoes
a small handful of fresh
  coriander leaves

1 Place all the ingredients for the curry paste in a food processor and blitz to form a paste.

2 To marinate the meat, place the chicken in a bowl or freezer bag, pour on the paste, stir to coat and marinate for a few hours. Skip this step if you are short on time and prefer not to marinate the meat.

3 Preheat your slow cooker, following the manufacturer's instructions.

4 Put the chicken, curry paste, onion and stock in the slow cooker. Combine well. Season with salt and pepper.

5 Set to Low, cover and cook for 6 hours.

6 Serve with basmati rice or cauliflower rice and naan bread.

TOP TIP
I like to marinate the meat for at least 2 hours before placing in the slow cooker. You don't have to do this, but it does boost the flavour.

This delicious chicken stew is called *dakdoritang* in Korea. It has the comfort of an English-style stew, along with some tasty spices. This recipe uses Korean red-hot pepper paste (known as *gochujang*), which is available in most big supermarkets. If you can't find it, use a standard chilli paste. Serve the stew with rice or, if you are a mashed potato lover like my husband, creamy mashed potato.

Korean Chicken Stew

SERVES 4

NUTRITIONAL INFORMATION
PER SERVING
297 Kcals
8.9g fat
17g net carbohydrates
2.1g fibre
35g protein

INGREDIENTS
2 tbsp olive oil or coconut oil
750g boneless chicken, diced
   (leg, thigh or breast)
1 large onion, sliced
2 garlic cloves, crushed
6 new potatoes, halved
1 carrot, thickly sliced
½ tsp chilli flakes
3cm piece of fresh ginger,
   peeled and grated
3 tbsp dark soy sauce
2 tbsp rice wine
1–2 tbsp Korean red-hot
   pepper paste (*gochujang*)
400ml hot chicken stock
3–4 spring onions, finely
   chopped, to garnish
1 green chilli, thinly sliced,
   to garnish
salt and ground black pepper

1 Preheat your slow cooker, following the manufacturer's instructions.

2 If your slow cooker has a sauté option, you can use this; if not, use a sauté pan on your hob. Heat the olive oil or coconut oil, add the chicken and cook until brown. Place in the slow cooker (if you used a separate pan).

3 Add all the remaining ingredients, except the spring onions and green chilli, and season with salt and pepper.

4 Set to Low, cover and cook for 6–8 hours.

5 Garnish with the spring onions and green chilli, and serve with rice or mashed potato.

A quick and easy version of the traditional French favourite. It has a lovely delicate flavour that works well with mash and green vegetables, or you can serve it the way the French do and just have it with some crusty French bread!

Simple Coq au Vin

SERVES 4

NUTRITIONAL INFORMATION
PER SERVING
416 Kcals
10g fat
16g net carbohydrates
2.5g fibre
40g protein

INGREDIENTS
1–2 tsp olive oil or coconut oil
500g chicken drumsticks
   (thigh also works well here)
200g smoked bacon lardons
12 shallots, peeled and left
   whole or halved, or 1 onion,
   roughly chopped
2 carrots, cut into batons
3 garlic cloves, thickly sliced
350ml red wine
2 bay leaves
2 tsp thyme
350ml hot chicken or bone
   stock
120g button mushrooms,
   halved or quartered if large
1–2 tbsp cornflour (optional)
salt and ground black pepper

1 Preheat your slow cooker, following the manufacturer's instructions.

2 If your slow cooker has a sauté function, you can use this; if not, use a sauté pan on your hob. Heat the oil, then add the chicken and brown for a few minutes. Add the lardons and cook until they start to brown. Remove from the heat.

3 Add all ingredients to the slow cooker apart from the mushrooms and cornflour, making sure the stock is hot when adding as this will help maintain the right temperature. Season with salt and pepper.

4 Set to Low, cover and cook for 6–8 hours.

5 Remove the lid and add the mushrooms. If the sauce is too thin, mix the cornflour with a little water to form a paste. Pour this into the slow cooker and stir to incorporate.

6 Set to High, cover and cook for another 30 minutes.

7 Serve with creamy mash and green vegetables.

This has a real kick, but feel free to cut down on the spices if you want a milder version. You can serve it straight from the slow cooker or, if you prefer the more traditional dark and crispy chicken, you can pop it under the grill before serving. Serve it with green salad. Remember to plan ahead, as the chicken needs to marinate for a couple of hours before placing in the slow cooker.

Jerk Chicken

SERVES 6

NUTRITIONAL INFORMATION
PER SERVING
289 Kcals
9.3g fat
17g net carbohydrates
3.3g fibre
32g protein

INGREDIENTS
1.5kg chicken pieces
  (legs, breast or thigh)
2 red onions, sliced

FOR THE JERK SEASONING
2 garlic cloves, crushed
2cm piece of fresh ginger,
  peeled and crushed
2–3 red or green chillies,
  finely chopped (or to taste)
2 tbsp thyme
2 tsp rosemary
2 tsp ground allspice
1 tsp ground nutmeg
2 tsp ground cinnamon
1 tbsp paprika
½ tsp chilli powder
½ tsp ground ginger
2 tbsp coconut oil, melted
grated zest and juice of 1 lime
2 tbsp honey
salt and ground black pepper

1 Place all the jerk seasoning ingredients in a food processor and blitz until smooth.

2 Put the chicken pieces in a bowl, add the jerk seasoning and mix to thoroughly coat the chicken. Place in a freezer bag or cover the bowl, and leave to marinate in the fridge for at least 2 hours (it can be left overnight in the fridge).

3 When ready to cook, preheat your slow cooker following the manufacturer's instructions.

4 Place the sliced onions and 250ml water in the base of the slow cooker and add the marinated chicken pieces. Season with salt and pepper.

5 Set to High, cover and cook for 3–4 hours, until the chicken is cooked (the timing will depend on the size of the chicken pieces).

6 Remove from the slow cooker. If you want a darker chicken, place it under a hot grill for 5–10 minutes, turning the chicken regularly until you have achieved your desired colour and crispness.

7 Serve with green salad and lime wedges.

This is a great recipe for a delicious and wholesome casserole, perfect to fill your family with goodness. Serve with mashed potato and steamed green vegetables.

Rustic Chicken Casserole

SERVES 4–6

NUTRITIONAL
INFORMATION PER SERVING
(FOR 6 SERVINGS)
399 Kcals
7.9g fat
34g net carbohydrates
6g fibre
45g protein

INGREDIENTS
1 large onion, chopped
2 garlic cloves, crushed
2 celery sticks, chopped
2 carrots, sliced
1 sweet potato, peeled and
  diced
400g tin chopped tomatoes
  (or 4–6 ripe fresh tomatoes,
  chopped)
500g boneless chicken pieces
  (breast, leg or thigh)
100g smoked bacon lardons
  (optional)
75g red lentils, rinsed
500ml hot chicken stock
  (or use half wine, half stock)

2 tsp paprika
1 bay leaf
75g sweetcorn (tinned, or
  frozen and defrosted)
a small handful of freshly
  chopped parsley
salt and ground black pepper

1 Preheat your slow cooker, following the manufacturer's instructions.

2 Place all the ingredients except the sweetcorn and parsley in the slow cooker. Make sure the stock is hot when adding as this will help maintain the right temperature.

3 Set to Low, cover and cook for 6–8 hours, or if you want a faster meal, set to High and cook for 4–5 hours.

4 Remove the lid, add the sweetcorn and parsley (reserving a little to garnish), season to taste and cook for another 15 minutes on High. I normally do this as I am putting some vegetables on to steam.

5 Sprinkle with parsley and serve with steamed green vegetables and mashed potato.

This is basically an Italian chicken 'hunter's' casserole (*cacciatore* means 'hunter' in Italian). I love Italian flavours and this certainly delivers. As with all my chicken recipes, you can choose the cut of chicken you prefer to use. Thigh and leg meat have the best flavour, but I do appreciate children tend to prefer chicken breast. Serve with crusty bread and salad.

Chicken Cacciatore

SERVES 4

NUTRITIONAL INFORMATION
PER SERVING
401 Kcals
11g fat
14g net carbohydrates
4.7g fibre
45g protein

INGREDIENTS
2 tsp olive oil or butter
1kg chicken pieces
6 slices of prosciutto, chopped
1 large onion, diced
2 garlic cloves, crushed
2 peppers (red or yellow),
  deseeded and diced
1 carrot, diced
400g tin chopped tomatoes
2 tbsp sun-dried tomato purée
300ml red wine
½ tsp chilli flakes
2 tsp oregano
1 tsp thyme
50g black olives, pitted
a small handful of fresh basil
  and thyme sprigs
salt and ground black pepper

1 Preheat your slow cooker, following the manufacturer's instructions.

2 If your slow cooker has a sauté option, you can use this; if not, use a sauté pan on your hob. Heat the olive oil or butter, add the chicken and cook until brown. Place in the slow cooker (if you used a separate pan).

3 Add all the remaining ingredients apart from the mushrooms, olives and fresh herbs.

4 Set to Low, cover and cook for 6–8 hours.

5 Remove the lid and add the olives, basil and thyme. Cover and cook on High for another 30 minutes.

6 Serve with crusty bread and salad.

This is a wonderfully creamy chicken curry. You can of course adjust the spice levels to taste but this, for me, is medium in potency. I serve it with basmati rice, or cauliflower or broccoli rice.

Almond Butter Chicken Curry

SERVES 4

NUTRITIONAL INFORMATION
PER SERVING
367 Kcals
14g fat
11g net carbohydrates
6g fibre
37g protein

INGREDIENTS
3cm piece of fresh ginger,
  peeled
3 garlic cloves, peeled
1–2 red or green chillies
  (to taste)
2 tsp coriander seeds
2 tsp ground coriander
2 tsp fenugreek seeds
1 tbsp garam masala
3 heaped tbsp smooth almond
  butter
5 tomatoes, quartered
500g boneless chicken (breast,
  leg or thigh), cut into large
  chunks
1 large onion, chopped
a small handful of fresh
  coriander leaves, chopped
grated zest of 1 lime
30g flaked almonds, toasted
  to garnish (optional)
salt and ground black pepper

1 Preheat your slow cooker, following the manufacturer's instructions.

2 Put the ginger, garlic, chillies and spices in a food processor with the almond butter and tomatoes and blitz to form a sauce.

3 Place the chicken in the slow cooker along with the onion. Add the sauce and combine well. Season with salt and pepper.

4 Set to Low, cover and cook for 6 hours, or if you want a faster meal, set to High and cook for 3–4 hours.

5 Remove the lid, add the fresh chopped coriander (reserving a little to garnish) and the lime zest, replace the lid and cook for a further 15 minutes on Low. If the curry is too thick, add a little water or chicken stock.

6 Stir and serve on a bed of rice. Garnish with the reserved coriander and toasted flaked almonds.

Stroganoff is usually made with beef and mushrooms, but this recipe uses chicken. I find chicken is preferable when cooking for younger children but just as tasty. Serve with mashed potato and steamed green vegetables.

Chicken Stroganoff

SERVES 4

NUTRITIONAL INFORMATION
PER SERVING
306 Kcals
12g fat
8.5g net carbohydrates
1.5g fibre
35g protein

INGREDIENTS
1 tsp coconut oil
500g boneless chicken, diced
   (breast, leg or thigh)
1 onion, finely chopped
2 garlic cloves, crushed
300g chestnut mushrooms,
   sliced
2–3 tsp paprika
150ml white wine
150ml hot chicken or
   bone stock
a small handful of fresh
   parsley leaves, chopped
2–3 tsp Dijon mustard
250g crème fraîche
1–2 tsp cornflour (optional)
salt and ground black pepper

1 Preheat your slow cooker, following the manufacturer's instructions.

2 If your slow cooker has a sauté function, you can use this; if not, use a sauté pan on your hob. Heat the coconut oil, add the chicken and sauté until brown. Place in the slow cooker (if you used a separate pan).

3 Add all remaining ingredients, except the parsley, mustard and crème fraiche, and season with salt and pepper.

4 Set to Low, cover and cook for 5–6 hours.

5 Remove the lid and stir in the parsley, mustard and crème fraîche to form a creamy sauce.

6 If it is too runny, mix the cornflour with a little water to form a paste. Add this to the slow cooker, cover, turn to High and cook for a further 15–20 minutes until it thickens.

7 Serve with mashed potato and steamed green vegetables.

Beef

Beef works really well in the slow cooker. The slow cooker is ideal for cheaper cuts of meat that would be quite tough unless cooked long and slow – I have mentioned some below, but if in doubt speak to your local butcher for more advice.

Most of the recipes in this chapter require stewing beef, which is also known as braising steak. You can also use brisket, which is a tad more fatty but still an excellent and economical choice for slow cooking. Oxtail needs long cooking to make it really tender. The flavours are often enhanced when eaten the day after cooking.

Minced meat is not generally suitable for long cooks, but it works well in the slow cooker if you cook it for a reduced time.

All beef recipes offer the option of sautéing the meat prior to slow cooking. This helps to enhance the flavour and colour of the dish.

This rich casserole bursts with flavour. It's a great family meal, and is also ideal for a dinner party, served with parsnip or celeriac mash and steamed green vegetables. Oxtail is an inexpensive but very flavoursome cut. Get your butcher to prepare the oxtail and cut it into pieces for you.

Rich Oxtail Casserole

SERVES 6

NUTRITIONAL INFORMATION
PER SERVING
519 Kcals
22g fat
19g net carbohydrates
4.9g fibre
41g protein

INGREDIENTS
1 tbsp plain flour
4 tsp paprika
1kg oxtail, cut into chunks
2 tsp olive oil or coconut oil
150g smoked back bacon,
  thickly diced, or smoked
  bacon lardons
3 garlic cloves, crushed
2 red onions, diced
2 carrots, diced
2 celery sticks, diced
1 large parsnip, peeled
  and diced
250ml red wine (ideally
  Burgundy or Rioja)
175ml port
3 tbsp tomato purée

1 beef stock cube
  (I use a beef stock pot)
2 tsp thyme
2 tsp parsley
1 tsp rosemary
2 bay leaves
salt and ground black pepper

1 Preheat your slow cooker, following the manufacturer's instructions.

2 Combine the flour and paprika in a bowl. Lightly coat the oxtail in the flour.

3 If your slow cooker has a sauté option, you can use this; if not, use a sauté pan on your hob. Heat the olive oil or coconut oil, add the oxtail and bacon and cook until brown. Place in the slow cooker (if you used a separate pan), including any juices.

4 Add the remaining ingredients to the slow cooker and season with salt and pepper.

5 Set to Low, cover and cook for 8 hours, until the oxtail meat comes away from the bone easily.

6 Remove the bay leaves. Serve with parsnip or celeriac mash and steamed green vegetables.

This recipe uses venison but you can use beef if you prefer – beef is a cheaper opton but just as flavoursome. This is a very tasty and rich, tender, meaty ragout. Serve with celeriac mash and steamed green vegetables.

Venison and Liver Ragout

SERVES 4

NUTRITIONAL INFORMATION
PER SERVING
500 Kcals
16g fat
17g net carbohydrates
4.4g fibre
56g protein

INGREDIENTS
1 tsp coconut oil (optional)
500g venison, diced
300g calf's liver, diced
200g smoked bacon lardons,
  diced
2–3 garlic cloves, chopped
2 onions, diced
400g tin chopped tomatoes
2 tbsp tomato purée
1 tsp thyme
1 bay leaf
1 tbsp Worcestershire sauce
300ml red wine
1 beef stock (I use a beef
  stock pot)
salt and ground black pepper
chopped fresh parsley, to
  garnish

1 Preheat your slow cooker, following the manufacturer's instructions.

2 Brown the meat, if you like. If your slow cooker has a sauté function, you can use this; if not, use a sauté pan on your hob. Heat the coconut oil, add the venison, liver and bacon and cook until brown. Place in the slow cooker (if you used a separate pan).

3 Add all the remaining ingredients to the slow cooker, combine well and season with salt and pepper.

4 Set to Low, cover and cook for 6–8 hours, until the venison and liver are very tender. Remove the bay leaf.

5 Serve with mash and green vegetables.

This is a traditional family favourite, made with good-quality mince. You can use stewing steak if you prefer, but increase the cooking time to 5–6 hours on Low. Serve with grated cheese and basmati rice or – for a low-calorie and low-carb option – cauliflower rice, along with a dollop of sour cream.

Chilli Con Carne

SERVES 4

NUTRITIONAL INFORMATION
PER SERVING
398 Kcals
9.2g fat
22g net carbohydrates
8.7g fibre
50g protein

INGREDIENTS
1 tsp olive oil or coconut oil
1 large red onion, finely
 chopped
2 star anise
2 garlic cloves, crushed
750g minced beef
250ml hot bone or beef stock
2 red peppers, deseeded
 and sliced
1–2 red or green chillies,
 chopped (to taste)
400g tin chopped tomatoes
200g tin red kidney beans,
 drained
200g butter beans, drained
3 tbsp tomato purée
1 tsp chilli powder
1 tsp ground cumin

1 heaped tsp smoked paprika
2 tsp paprika
1½ tsp marjoram
1–2 squares dark chocolate
 (95% cocoa solids)
80g chestnut mushrooms,
 quartered
salt and ground black pepper

1 Preheat your slow cooker, following the manufacturer's instructions.

2 If your slow cooker has a sauté option, you can use this; if not, use a sauté pan on your hob. Heat the oil, add the onion, star anise and garlic and sauté for a couple of minutes. Add the beef and cook until brown. Remove the star anise. Place the beef, onion and garlic in the slow cooker (if you used a separate pan).

3 Add all the remaining ingredients, except the chocolate, and season with salt and pepper.

4 Set to Low, cover and cook for 4 hours. Half an hour before serving, remove the lid and stir in the chocolate and mushrooms.

5 Serve with grated cheese and basmati rice or cauliflower rice, and sour cream on the side.

Bourbon goes really well with beef and adds a different flavour to using red wine or port. As the name suggests, this is a very rich and smoky beef dish, perfect for family meals or dinner parties. Serve with buttery mashed potato or celeriac mash, and steamed green leafy vegetables.

Rich and Smoky Bourbon Beef

SERVES 6

NUTRITIONAL INFORMATION
PER SERVING
577 Kcals
26g fat
16g net carbohydrates
3g fibre
37g protein

INGREDIENTS
1–2 tbsp plain flour
750g stewing beef, cut into
  chunks
2 tsp olive oil or coconut oil
200g thick smoked pancetta,
  diced
1 red onion, diced
1 red pepper, deseeded and
  thickly sliced
2 garlic cloves, roughly
  chopped
400g tin chopped tomatoes
2 tbsp sun-dried tomato paste
300ml bourbon
1 tsp thyme
½ tsp rosemary
2 tsp marjoram

½ tsp cayenne pepper
2 tbsp smoked paprika
1 tsp ground cumin
2 tbsp honey
2 bay leaves
1 beef stock cube
  (I use a beef stock pot)
salt and ground black pepper

1 Place the flour in a bowl, add the beef and toss to coat it with the flour.

2 If your slow cooker has a sauté function, you can use this; if not, use a frying pan or sauté pan on your hob. Heat the oil, add the beef and cook until brown. Add the pancetta and cook for a couple of minutes. Place in the slow cooker (if you used a separate pan).

3 Add all the remaining ingredients to the slow cooker, stir and season with salt and pepper.

4 Set to Low, cover and cook for 6–8 hours. Remove the bay leaves before serving.

5 Serve with mashed potato or celeriac mash and steamed green vegetables.

Don't let the long ingredients list for this traditional Malaysian beef curry put you off – it is so easy to make, flavoursome and impressive. Just like other curries and spicy dishes, this rendang improves with time, so it's often best on the second day! Serve the curry with basmati or Thai rice.

Fragrant Rendang Curry

SERVES 6

NUTRITIONAL INFORMATION
PER SERVING
381 Kcals
22g fat
12g net carbohydrates
3.9g fibre
31g protein

INGREDIENTS
2 tsp coconut oil
750g stewing beef, diced
1 large red onion, roughly
  diced
2 red peppers, deseeded and
  cut into large chunks
30g coconut flakes, to garnish
1 red chilli thinly sliced,
  to garnish
fresh coriander leaves,
  to garnish
→

1 Place all the curry paste ingredients in a food processor and blitz until they form a smooth paste.

2 Preheat your slow cooker, following the manufacturer's instructions.

3 If your slow cooker has a sauté option, you can use this; if not, use a sauté pan on your hob. Heat the coconut oil, add the beef and cook until brown. Place in the slow cooker (if you used a separate pan).

4 Add the curry paste, onion and peppers, and stir. Season with salt and pepper.

5 Set to Low, cover and cook for 8 hours.

6 Just before serving, toast the coconut flakes: place them in a dry frying pan over a medium heat and cook until they start to brown, moving them continually to prevent them burning.

7 Sprinkle the curry with coconut flakes, chilli and coriander and serve with basmati or Thai rice.

TOP TIP
Double up the curry paste and store it in the freezer, ready to use whenever you fancy a curry.

FOR THE CURRY PASTE

4cm piece of fresh ginger,
  peeled
4 garlic cloves, peeled and
  left whole
3 red or green chillies
  (or to taste)
2 lemongrass stalks, remove
  hard outer layers
4cm piece of fresh galangal
4 whole cardamom pods
4 kaffir lime leaves
  (fresh or dried)
1 tsp fennel seeds
2 tsp coriander seeds
1 tsp cumin seeds
grated zest and juice of 1 lime
2 tsp ground cinnamon
½ tsp ground ginger
1 tsp hot paprika
1 tsp ground turmeric
1 tbsp honey
400ml tin coconut milk
salt and ground black pepper

This dish is perfect for dinner parties as you can prepare it in advance and enjoy being a host while it cooks, making everything look effortless. Preparing it the day before is worthwhile – it really improves with time! Serve with mashed potato or celeriac mash and steamed green leafy vegetables.

Beef Bourguignon

SERVES 6

NUTRITIONAL INFORMATION
PER SERVING
433 Kcals
20g fat
10g net carbohydrates
2.9g fibre
38g protein

INGREDIENTS
1–2 tbsp plain flour
750g stewing beef, diced
2 tsp olive oil or coconut oil
200g thick smoked pancetta,
  diced
1 small red onion, diced
2 garlic cloves, roughly
  chopped
200g shallots, peeled
1 carrot, diced
1 celery stick, diced
400g tin chopped tomatoes
400ml red wine (Burgundy)
1 tsp thyme
½ tsp rosemary
2 heaped tsp paprika
1 beef stock cube
  (I use a beef stock pot)
150g button mushrooms
salt and ground black pepper

1 Place the flour in a bowl, add the beef and toss to coat it with the flour.

2 If your slow cooker has a sauté function, you can use this; if not, use a frying pan or sauté pan on your hob. Heat the oil, add the beef and cook until brown. Add the pancetta and brown for a couple of minutes. Place in the slow cooker (if you used a separate pan).

3 Add all the remaining ingredients, except the mushrooms, to the slow cooker and combine well. Season with salt and pepper.

4 Set to Low, cover and cook for 7–8 hours.

5 Remove the lid and add the mushrooms, stirring well so they are submerged. Set to High, cover and cook for a further 30 minutes.

6 Serve with mashed potato or celeriac mash and steamed vegetables.

My dad loved a steak and kidney pudding. Offal is bursting with nutrients, especially protein, omega-3 fatty acids, B vitamins, zinc and iron, and it is very economical. Traditionally, steak and kidney pudding would just be made with steak, kidney and an onion, but I like to add some vegetables, herbs and spices to enhance its flavour. Serve the pudding with steamed green vegetables.

Steak and Kidney Pudding

SERVES 4

NUTRITIONAL INFORMATION
PER SERVING
655 Kcals
30 g fat
15g net carbohydrates
4g fibre
42g protein

EQUIPMENT
You will need a 1.2-litre pudding bowl, baking parchment, foil and string (I like to use double-sided parchment from Lakeland, with foil on one side and parchment on the other).

INGREDIENTS
butter or lard, for greasing
1 tbsp plain flour
2 tsp paprika
½ tsp mustard powder
500g stewing beef, diced
2 tsp olive oil
150g kidney, thickly diced (lamb, beef, or ox)
1 large red onion, diced
1 carrot, finely diced
→

1 Grease the pudding bowl thoroughly and generously with butter or lard and set to one side. You can place a circle of baking parchment in the base of the bowl if you are worried about the pudding sticking.

2 To make the suet pastry, combine the flour and suet in a bowl and add up to 150ml cold water (you may not need it all), a little at a time, combining with a knife or your hands until you form a nice dough.

3 Dust your work surface with flour and roll the dough to approximately 5mm thickness. Use the top rim of your pudding bowl as a template to cut out a circle for the lid of the pie and place to one side. Use the remaining pastry to line the pudding bowl.

4 Preheat your slow cooker, following the manufacturer's instructions.

5 Combine the flour, paprika and mustard powder in a bowl, add the beef and ensure it is well coated with the flour.

6 Heat the olive oil in a large frying pan or sauté pan and add the meat, including the kidney. Fry gently over a medium heat until brown. Add all the remaining ingredients, except the stock, to the pan, combine well and season with salt and pepper. Remove from the heat.

7 Carefully spoon the meat mixture into the lined pudding bowl. Carefully pour in the hot stock until it covers around three quarters of the meat (do not overfill it).

½ tsp marjoram
½ tsp thyme
175ml hot bone or beef stock
salt and ground black pepper

FOR THE SUET PASTRY
225g self-raising flour, plus
  extra for dusting
100g shredded beef suet

8 Use a pastry brush to gently brush some water around the edges of the pudding pastry and the base of the pastry lid. Place the lid over the bowl and seal the edges well.

9 Cover the pudding bowl with baking parchment, pleating it at the centre to allow for expansion, then add a pleated layer of foil and tie very securely with string. Make a handle with string or foil to make it easier to lift the pudding in and out of the slow cooker (see page 153).

10 Boil the kettle. Place the pudding in the base of your slow cooker. Add boiling water to the slow cooker until it comes halfway up the sides of the pudding bowl.

11 Set to High, cover and cook for 4–5 hours, or set to Low, cover and cook for 6–8 hours.

12 Remove the pudding bowl from the slow cooker using your string or foil to lift it out. Remove the foil and parchment. Place a plate on the top of the bowl and flip the bowl and plate over so the suet pudding drops onto the plate.

13 Serve with steamed green vegetables.

TOP TIP
For extra flavour and richness, swap the stock for stout.

I remember when I first cooked a joint of beef – I was so nervous! It didn't help that my family couldn't agree about how well done it should be.

Using a slow cooker makes a deliciously tender joint of beef, and it's also really useful as it frees up space in your oven for all the other Sunday roast favourites. Serve with roast potatoes, Yorkshire puddings and a selection of vegetables. Remember to retain the juices to use in your gravy!

Simple Slow-cooked Beef Roast

SERVES 6

NUTRITIONAL INFORMATION
PER SERVING
269 Kcals
9.6g fat
3.9g net carbohydrates
1.6g fibre
41g protein

INGREDIENTS
1 large onion, cut into wedges
2 carrots, cut into thick batons
3 tbsp wholegrain mustard
1kg beef roasting joint
500ml hot bone or beef stock
salt and ground black pepper

1 Preheat your slow cooker, following the manufacturer's instructions.

2 Place the onion and carrots into the base of your slow cooker.

3 Rub the mustard over the top of the beef joint.

4 Place the beef on the bed of vegetables in the slow cooker and pour the stock around the joint.

5 Set to Low, cover and cook for 3–4 hours, depending on how well done you like your beef. You can check your beef is done by piercing it with a skewer: the juices should run red for rare, pink for medium and clear for well-done.

6 Remove the beef from the slow cooker and place it on a carving board. Cover with foil and allow to rest for at least 15 minutes.

7 Drain the stock from the slow cooker and use some of this to make your gravy.

8 Serve with roast potatoes, Yorkshire puddings and vegetables.

TOP TIP
For crispy roast potatoes, peel and cut potatoes at an angle (keep them quite large). Place a roasting tray in the oven with your chosen fat (ideally goose fat, beef dripping or olive oil). Boil the potatoes in water for 10 minutes, drain thoroughly and shake gently to fluff up the potatoes. Place in the hot roasting tray and turn until all sides are coated in the fat. Sprinkle with paprika and roast in a hot oven for 1 hour, or until golden.

Beef works brilliantly with Guinness or stout. You can also use real ale. I use a beef stock pot to add some more beefy flavour, as I find they provide more flavour than a dry stock cube, but it is up to you which you use. This is lovely served with parsnip or celeriac mash and steamed green vegetables.

Beef and Guinness Casserole with Thyme Dumplings

SERVES 6

NUTRITIONAL INFORMATION
PER SERVING
427 Kcals
15g fat
25g net carbohydrates
3.5g fibre
41g protein

INGREDIENTS
1 heaped tbsp plain flour
2–3 tsp paprika (to taste)
2 tsp olive oil or coconut oil
1kg stewing beef, diced
1 red onion, finely chopped
1 leek, trimmed and thinly
  sliced
2 carrots, cut into chunks
2 parsnips, peeled and thickly
  sliced
500ml Guinness or stout
1 bay leaf
1 beef stock cube
  (I use a beef stock pot)
salt and ground black pepper

FOR THE THYME DUMPLINGS
150g self-raising flour
70g beef suet
2 tsp thyme

1 Combine the flour and paprika in a bowl, add the diced beef and toss to coat.

2 If your slow cooker has a sauté function, you can use this; if not, use a sauté pan on your hob. Heat the olive oil or coconut oil, add the beef and cook until brown. Place in the slow cooker (if you used a separate pan).

3 Add all the remaining stew ingredients (not the dumpling mixture) and season with salt and pepper.

4 Set to Low, cover and cook for 6–7 hours. Remove the bay leaf.

5 An hour before the casserole is ready, make the dumpling dough. Mix the flour, suet and thyme together in a bowl. Add 3 tablespoons of cold water a little at a time, stirring until the mixture forms a nice dough that's not too wet. Work the dough into 6–8 small balls and place them on top of the casserole. Set the slow cooker to High and cook for a further 30 minutes–1 hour, until the dumplings fluff up. If you want to bake the dumplings instead, follow the tip below.

6 Serve the casserole and dumplings with steamed green vegetables.

TOP TIP
If you like crispy dumplings rather than the doughy kind, cook them in the oven instead of with the casserole. Simply place the dumplings in a greased muffin tin (one dumpling per muffin hole) and bake in the oven at 190°C (170°C fan oven) Gas 5 for 15–20 minutes until golden and crisp.

This very simple beef casserole has a lovely warming hit of horseradish and mustard. It's so easy and perfect for winter evenings.

Beef and Horseradish Stew

SERVES 6

NUTRITIONAL INFORMATION
PER SERVING
309 Kcals
10g fat
12g net carbohydrates
1.7g fibre
42g protein

INGREDIENTS
2 tbsp plain flour or cornflour
1 tsp paprika
½ tsp ground ginger
1kg stewing beef, diced
1 tsp olive oil or coconut oil
400g baby onions or shallots,
  peeled
2 garlic cloves, finely chopped
500ml hot bone or beef stock
200g chestnut mushrooms,
  thickly sliced or quartered
2 tbsp Dijon mustard
3 tbsp creamed horseradish
  sauce
salt and ground black pepper

1 Preheat your slow cooker, following the manufacturer's instructions.

2 Combine the flour, paprika and ginger in a bowl, add the diced beef and toss to coat.

3 If your slow cooker has a sauté function, you can use this; if not, use a sauté pan on your hob. Heat the olive oil or coconut oil, add the beef and cook until brown. Place in the slow cooker (if you used a separate pan).

4 Add the onions, garlic and stock to the slow cooker and season with salt and pepper.

5 Set to Low, cover and cook for 6–8 hours.

6 Half an hour before the end of the cooking time, remove the lid, add the mushrooms, mustard and horseradish, and stir well until combined. Set to High, cover and cook for 30 minutes, until the mushrooms are cooked.

7 Serve with green vegetables and creamy mash.

Pork

The recipes in this chapter use pork, ham, gammon and bacon. They all work well in the slow cooker and have the advantage of being cheap to buy and surprisingly healthy meats that are high in protein, iron and B vitamins. When buying bacon, gammon and ham, ensure you choose the most unprocessed, best-quality meat you can find.

You can buy lots of different cuts of pork that work well in the slow cooker: I mostly use pork belly, tenderloins, cheek and shoulder. Hocks are particularly economical and tasty, and they cook nicely in the slow cooker – cook them in a similar way to cooking a ham or gammon joint (see page 182). Speak to your butcher about other low-cost cuts that are suitable for slow cooking.

This is a lovely dish. Despite being a one-pot meal, it is wonderful even in the summer months thanks to its delicious flavours. This is quite a filling recipe so it doesn't need any accompaniment other than some fresh, crusty bread.

Chorizo and Bean Tuscan-style Pork

SERVES 4

NUTRITIONAL INFORMATION
PER SERVING
673 Kcals
43g fat
27g net carbohydrates
9g fibre
39g protein

INGREDIENTS
2 tsp olive oil or coconut oil
500g pork shoulder, diced
110g cooking chorizo, cut into
  thick slices (skin removed)
3 garlic cloves, crushed
1 large red onion, finely
  chopped
2 red peppers, deseeded and
  thickly diced
1 celery stick, diced
1 carrot, diced
400g tin chopped tomatoes
3 tbsp sun-dried tomato paste
400g tin cannellini beans,
  drained
300ml hot bone, pork or
  chicken stock

3 tsp oregano
1 tsp rosemary
½ tsp basil
½ tsp marjoram
½ tsp sage
1 tsp parsley
salt and ground black pepper
flat-leaf parsley, chopped,
  to garnish

1 Preheat your slow cooker, following the manufacturer's instructions.

2 If your slow cooker has a sauté function, you can use this; if not, use a sauté pan on your hob. Heat the olive oil or coconut oil, add the diced pork and chorizo and cook until brown. Place in the slow cooker (if you used a separate pan).

3 Add all the remaining ingredients to the slow cooker, stir, and season with salt and pepper.

4 Set to Low, cover and cook for 7–8 hours.

5 Serve with fresh, crusty bread.

My son loves pulled pork stuffed in a wrap (it also works well in buns), so this recipe gets cooked quite regularly in my house. I am not keen on a very sweet sauce with pulled pork, but if you are, add another 1–2 tablespoons of honey.

Pulled Pork

SERVES 6

NUTRITIONAL INFORMATION
PER SERVING
490 Kcals
28g fat
21g net carbohydrates
1.6g fibre
32g protein

INGREDIENTS
1kg pork shoulder, excess fat
  and skin removed (this can
  be used for pork crackling)
300ml bone, pork or chicken
  stock
2 garlic cloves
50ml apple cider vinegar
50ml balsamic vinegar
50ml brandy or whisky
1 tbsp smoked paprika
1 tbsp mild chilli powder
2 tbsp honey
1 tsp thyme
1 tsp marjoram
½ tsp ground ginger
½ tsp ground cinnamon
2 tbsp Worcestershire sauce
200ml barbecue sauce
salt and ground black pepper

1 Preheat your slow cooker, following the manufacturer's instructions.

2 Place the pork shoulder in the base of your slow cooker.

3 Put the remaining ingredients in a food processor with some salt and pepper and blitz until smooth. Pour the sauce over the pork.

4 Set the slow cooker to Low, cover and cook for 6–8 hours.

5 When ready to serve, remove the pork and using two forks pull the pork apart. You can place the pulled pork back in the slow cooker to mix with a small amount of the remaining sauce if you wish. Stuff the pulled pork into wraps or buns, to serve.

This is a lovely dinner for all the family, and as it's mild and sweet, it's great for helping to get young children used to different flavours. You don't have to use pork for this dish; you could opt for chicken or turkey if you wish. Serve with basmati or brown rice.

Sweet and Sour Pork

SERVES 4

NUTRITIONAL INFORMATION
PER SERVING
488 Kcals
20g fat
40g net carbohydrates
2.9g fibre
28g protein

INGREDIENTS
500g pork fillet or loin,
  cubed or cut into strips
1 onion, chopped
3 garlic cloves, crushed
1 yellow pepper, deseeded
  and diced
1 red pepper, deseeded
  and diced
2–3cm piece of fresh ginger,
  peeled and finely chopped
100ml white wine
75ml red wine vinegar
3–4 tbsp honey (to taste)
300g tin pineapple chunks,
  including natural juice
3–4 tbsp soy sauce (to taste)
2 tbsp tomato ketchup
2–3 heaped tsp cornflour
  (optional)
salt and ground black pepper

1 Preheat your slow cooker, following the manufacturer's instructions.

2 Place all the ingredients, except the cornflour, in the slow cooker, stir and season with salt and pepper.

3 Set to Low, cover and cook for 6–8 hours.

4 Check the pork after 6–8 hours and if you prefer a thicker sauce, mix the cornflour with a little water to form a paste, then stir it into the pork mix. Set to High, cover and cook for a further 30 minutes.

5 Serve the pork on a bed of rice.

Growing up, my uncle and aunt had a farm where my brother and I spent much of our childhood. One of the many wonderful things about staying at the farm was that we celebrated the seasons. Every autumn, we would get together for a bonfire. My aunt used to cook a lovely, hearty sausage casserole, perfect after an evening spent running around. This is my version, which I serve with cheesy mash and steamed shredded savoy cabbage.

Sausage and Bean Casserole

SERVES 4

NUTRITIONAL INFORMATION
PER SERVING
500 Kcals
30g fat
25g net carbohydrates
7.4g fibre
29g protein

INGREDIENTS
1 tsp olive oil or coconut oil
8 good-quality thick pork
  sausages
150g thick smoked bacon
  lardons
2 garlic cloves, crushed
1 onion, diced
1 red pepper, deseeded and
  thickly diced
400g tin chopped tomatoes
2 x 400g tins cannellini beans,
  drained
2 tsp sweet paprika
2 tsp oregano
300ml hot bone or chicken
  stock
salt and ground black pepper

1 Preheat your slow cooker, following the manufacturer's instructions.

2 If your slow cooker has a sauté function, you can use this; if not, use a sauté pan on your hob. Heat the olive oil or coconut oil, add the sausages and lardons and cook until brown all over. Place in the slow cooker (if you used a separate pan).

3 Add all the remaining ingredients, stir and season with salt and pepper.

4 Set to Low, cover and cook for 6–8 hours.

5 Serve the casserole with mash and shredded steamed cabbage.

TOP TIP
Vegetarians can swap the pork sausages for vegetarian ones and omit the lardons.

If you have not used fennel before, I urge you to give it a try. It works perfectly with pork to create a gorgeous casserole which is delicious at any time of the year. I like to serve this with parsnip mash and steamed green vegetables.

Pork and Fennel Casserole

SERVES 4

NUTRITIONAL INFORMATION PER SERVING
456 Kcals
32.7g fat
3.7g net carbohydrates
1.7g fibre
36.7g protein

INGREDIENTS
1 tsp olive oil or coconut oil
750g diced pork shoulder
1 onion, diced
2 garlic cloves, crushed
1 fennel bulb, thinly sliced
1 tsp rosemary
2 tsp oregano
1 tsp thyme
300ml hot bone, chicken or
   pork stock
salt and ground black pepper

1 Preheat your slow cooker, following the manufacturer's instructions.

2 If your slow cooker has a sauté function, you can use this; if not, use a sauté pan on your hob. Heat the olive oil or coconut oil, add the pork and cook until brown. Place in the slow cooker (if you used a separate pan).

3 Add all the remaining ingredients to the slow cooker, stir and season with salt and pepper.

4 Set to Low, cover and cook for 6–8 hours.

5 Serve with parsnip mash and green vegetables.

This is a really tasty way to cook pork, ensuring it is tender and juicy. I like to make this in the slow cooker in the summer, especially if we're having a barbecue. I can cook this in the slow cooker and finish it off on the barbecue for 5 minutes at the end, to help brown the pork before serving it with even more sticky sauce.

Sticky Pork

SERVES 4

NUTRITIONAL INFORMATION
PER SERVING
493 Kcals
26g fat
29g net carbohydrates
0g fibre
36g protein

INGREDIENTS
2 tsp olive oil or coconut oil
700g pork ribs or pork loin,
  thickly sliced
2 tbsp Worcestershire sauce
4 tbsp soy sauce
6 tbsp honey
grated zest and juice of 1 lime
2cm piece of fresh ginger,
  peeled and grated
2 garlic cloves, crushed
2 tsp Chinese five-spice
salt and ground black pepper
2 tsp cornflour (optional)

1 Preheat your slow cooker, following the manufacturer's instructions.

2 If your slow cooker has a sauté function, you can use this; if not, use a sauté pan on your hob. Heat the olive oil or coconut oil, add the pork and cook until brown. Place in the slow cooker (if you used a separate pan). You can skip this step if you prefer.

3 Mix the remaining ingredients, except the cornflour, in a bowl and season with salt and pepper. Pour this sauce over the pork.

4 Set to Low, cover and cook for 6–8 hours.

5 Remove the pork from the slow cooker. Pour the sauce into a saucepan. If you want to make the sauce thicker, mix the cornflour with a little water to form a paste and stir it into the sauce. Cook over a medium heat until it has thickened.

6 Place the pork on a serving plate with the sauce in a jug.

Pork and apple go together so well. This recipe is an absolute delight – so sweet and flavoursome. Speak to your butcher about the best cuts of meat for casseroles: here, I've used pork shoulder but you can also use pork cheeks, pork belly or tenderloin. Celeriac mash and steamed green vegetables make perfect accompaniments.

Pork, Cider and Apple Casserole

SERVES 6

NUTRITIONAL INFORMATION PER SERVING

424 Kcals
17g fat
28g net carbohydrates
4.6g fibre
35g protein

INGREDIENTS

2 tbsp plain flour
750g pork shoulder, diced
2 tsp olive oil or butter
200g thick smoked lardons, diced
1 large onion, sliced
1 celery stick, diced
2 carrots, diced
1 large parsnip, peeled and diced
1 bay leaf
½ tsp tarragon
350ml dry cider
1 pork or chicken stock cube (I use a pork or chicken stock pot)
3 apples, cored and quartered (skins on)
3 tbsp crème fraîche
1 tbsp wholegrain mustard
salt and ground black pepper

1 Preheat your slow cooker, following the manufacturer's instructions.

2 Put the flour in a bowl, add the pork and toss to coat.

3 If your slow cooker has a sauté function, you can use this; if not, use a sauté pan on your hob. Heat the olive oil or butter, add the pork and bacon and cook until brown. Place in the slow cooker (if you used a separate pan).

4 Add the remaining ingredients to the slow cooker, except the crème fraîche and mustard, and season with salt and pepper.

5 Set to Low, cover and cook for 6–8 hours. Remove the bay leaf.

6 Add the crème fraîche and mustard, set to High, cover and cook for a further 15 minutes.

7 Serve with celeriac mash and steamed green vegetables.

This is a really easy way to make a simple, tender, slow-cooked pork belly, ready to serve with steamed vegetables or whatever you choose. It is a two-step process: for best results, finish the belly in the oven or on the hob to brown before serving.

Slow-cooked Pork Belly

SERVES 6

NUTRITIONAL INFORMATION
PER SERVING
471 Kcals
34g fat
5.4g net carbohydrates
1.1g fibre
32g protein

INGREDIENTS
1 lemon, sliced
2 garlic cloves, crushed
2 onions, sliced
300ml dry cider
1kg pork belly
salt and ground black pepper

1 Preheat your slow cooker, following the manufacturer's instructions.

2 Place the lemon, garlic and onions in the base of the slow cooker then add the cider.

3 Place the pork belly on top of the onions and garlic, skin side up, and season with salt and pepper.

4 Set to Low, cover and cook for 6–8 hours.

5 Preheat your oven to 200°C (180°C fan oven) Gas 6.

6 Remove the pork from the slow cooker and transfer it to a non-stick baking tray. Place in the oven and cook for 20 minutes, until the skin has browned. If you want a very crisp crackling, cook it for a little longer.

7 Serve immediately with steamed vegetables and roast potatoes.

Lamb

Lamb works brilliantly in the slow cooker, benefiting from the long, slow cook which makes the meat beautifully tender and flavoursome. You can use leg, breast, loin, neck, shoulder, saddle or rump. As with any meat, ask your butcher to recommend the best cuts of lamb for your chosen dish.

You will find recipes for lamb shanks, lamb chops and hotpot in this chapter. Lamb shanks are one of my favourites — they are truly delicious when slowly cooked. You can also use diced lamb for casserole, ragout, curry and tagine dishes.

It is worth investing in some good-quality lamb stock cubes or stock pots if you don't make your own stock. I make my own bone broth (see page 199) and store it in the freezer.

What can be more traditional for the slow cooker than a lovely Lancashire hotpot? I have tweaked this to make it a little richer and more flavoursome than a typical hotpot. This is a family favourite that is cheap to make but really satisfying and tasty, and works well served alongside shredded steamed savoy cabbage.

Rich Lancashire Hotpot

SERVES 6

NUTRITIONAL INFORMATION
PER SERVING
414 Kcals
14g fat
29g net carbohydrates
5.1g fibre
36g protein

INGREDIENTS
2 tbsp plain flour
1 tsp paprika
750g stewing lamb, diced
1 tbsp olive oil or butter
2 onions, finely chopped
3 carrots, cut into chunks
1 celery stick, chopped
2–3 potatoes, peeled and sliced
2 lamb kidneys, diced
  (about 250g)
100ml red wine
350ml hot bone, lamb or
  chicken stock
2 tsp thyme
2 tsp rosemary
2 tsp mint sauce
1 tbsp Worcestershire sauce
salt and ground black pepper
grated cheese, to serve
  (optional)

1 Preheat your slow cooker, following the manufacturer's instructions.

2 Combine the flour and paprika in a bowl, add the diced lamb and toss to coat.

3 If your slow cooker has a sauté function, you can use this; if not, use a sauté pan on your hob. Heat the olive oil or butter, add the diced lamb and cook until brown. Place in the slow cooker (if you used a separate pan).

4 Add the onions, carrots, celery and kidneys to the slow cooker, season with salt and pepper before finishing with the sliced potato.

5 Mix the wine and stock with the herbs, mint sauce and Worcestershire sauce. Pour this over the lamb, vegetables and potato slices.

6 Set to Low, cover and cook for 7–8 hours. Sometimes the potatoes can go a bit grey if they are not in contact with enough of the liquid. If you see this happening, just dunk them a little to moisten them. You can, if you wish, submerge them completely into the hotpot.

7 If you want to brown the potatoes before serving, remove the lid and place the inner slow cooker bowl (if you can) under a hot grill. For added flavour, sprinkle over some grated cheese before grilling.

8 Serve with shredded steamed cabbage.

I love spicy food, but this Moroccan lamb has more of a delicate heat so is suitable for those who prefer a milder hit of chilli. I serve this dish with giant couscous and some flatbreads.

Moroccan Spiced Lamb

SERVES 4

NUTRITIONAL INFORMATION PER SERVING
424 Kcals
16g fat
30g net carbohydrates
11g fibre
34g protein

INGREDIENTS
1 tsp olive oil or coconut oil
500g stewing lamb, diced
1 large red onion, diced
1 large carrot, diced
1–2 red or green chillies, finely chopped
2 celery sticks, diced
1 red or yellow pepper, deseeded and diced
2–3cm piece of fresh ginger, peeled and finely chopped
2 garlic cloves, roughly chopped
8–10 dried apricots, chopped
400g tin chickpeas, drained
3–4 tsp ras el hanout spice blend (to taste)
400ml hot bone, lamb or vegetable stock

20g flaked almonds
salt and ground black pepper
fresh pomegranate seeds, to garnish
fresh coriander leaves, to garnish

1 Preheat your slow cooker, following the manufacturer's instructions.

2 If your slow cooker has a sauté function, you can use this; if not, use a sauté pan on your hob. Heat the olive oil or coconut oil, add the diced lamb and cook until brown. Place in the slow cooker (if you used a separate pan).

3 Add all the remaining ingredients, except the flaked almonds. Season with salt and pepper.

4 Set to Low, cover and cook for 8 hours.

5 Just before serving, remove the lid and stir in the flaked almonds.

6 Serve sprinkled with pomegranate seeds and fresh coriander leaves, alongside giant couscous and flatbreads.

I have included this recipe in a couple of my other slow cooker cookbooks, but it really is a great family classic so it would seem wrong not to include here. It was my dad's favourite, especially when served with buttery mashed potato with a side of mint sauce.

Lamb Shanks

SERVES 4

NUTRITIONAL INFORMATION
PER SERVING
454 Kcals
23.4g fat
18.8g net carbohydrates
4.4g fibre
38g protein

INGREDIENTS
2 red onions, finely diced
3 garlic cloves, crushed
2 celery sticks, thinly sliced
1 leek, trimmed and thinly
  sliced
2 carrots, finely diced
4 lamb shanks
400g tin chopped tomatoes
2 tsp tomato purée
4 tsp balsamic vinegar
200ml red wine
200ml hot bone, lamb or
  vegetable stock
1 tsp paprika
1–2 tsp mint sauce
2 bay leaves
3 sprigs each of fresh thyme
  and rosemary
2–3 tsp cornflour (optional)
salt and ground black pepper
chopped fresh flat-leaf parsley,
  to garnish

1 Preheat your slow cooker, following the manufacturer's instructions.

2 Place all the ingredients in the slow cooker, stir to combine and make sure everything is evenly distributed.

3 Set the slow cooker to Low, cover and cook for 8–10 hours, until the lamb is tender. Remove the bay leaves.

4 Just before serving, if the liquid is too thin, mix the cornflour with a little water to make a paste, remove the lamb shanks, stir in the paste to form a thicker stock, and place the lamb shanks back in the slow cooker. Turn the heat to High to thicken for 5–10 minutes.

5 Season to taste with salt and pepper and sprinkle with chopped parsley before serving.

You may not have considered making a moussaka in the slow cooker, but it cooks beautifully. I often use beef mince instead of lamb as my son prefers the flavour. I love to serve this with a crunchy green salad.

Lamb Moussaka

SERVES 4

NUTRITIONAL INFORMATION
PER SERVING
679 Kcals
39g fat
36g net carbohydrates
8g fibre
42g protein

INGREDIENTS
2 aubergines, thickly sliced
2 tsp olive oil
1 red onion, finely chopped
2 garlic cloves, crushed
500g lean lamb mince
400g tin chopped tomatoes
1 heaped tbsp tomato purée
2 tsp ground cinnamon
1 tsp mint
2 tsp oregano
2 potatoes, peeled and thinly
   sliced
200ml hot bone or lamb stock
300g crème fraîche or cream
   cheese
2 eggs, beaten
75g mature Cheddar or
   Parmesan cheese, grated,
   plus extra for sprinkling
salt and ground black pepper

1 Place the aubergine slices on a tray and sprinkle them with salt. Set to one side.

2 Preheat your slow cooker, following the manufacturer's instructions.

3 Meanwhile, heat the olive oil in a large frying pan or sauté pan, add the onion and garlic and cook until softened. Add the lamb mince and cook until brown, breaking it up with a wooden spoon.

4 Add the chopped tomatoes and purée, cinnamon, mint and oregano and combine well. Season with salt and pepper and set to one side.

5 Rub or spray the inside of the stock pot with olive oil.

6 Rinse the aubergine gently under cold running water and pat the slices dry with kitchen towel.

7 Place half the mince in your slow cooker, followed by a layer of half the aubergine slices and then half the potato. Add another layer of mince and finish with a layer of the remaining potato and aubergine.

8 Set to Low, cover and cook for 4 hours.

9 An hour before the end of the cooking time, mix the crème fraîche or cream cheese with the eggs and grated cheese. Season with black pepper and pour over the moussaka. Sprinkle with Parmesan or Cheddar, cover and cook on High for another hour.

10 If you want the moussaka to have a golden top, place it under a hot grill for 5–10 minutes before serving.

This curry needs a long, slow cook to keep the lamb juicy and tender. Serve with some rice and naan or flatbreads for a delicious meal.

Lamb Balti

SERVES 4

NUTRITIONAL INFORMATION
PER SERVING
412 Kcals
18g fat
17g net carbohydrates
7.7g fibre
42g protein

INGREDIENTS
2 tsp olive oil or coconut oil
750g stewing lamb, diced
1 large red onion, roughly
　chopped
2 red peppers, deseeded and
　cut into large chunks
a handful of fresh coriander
　leaves, to garnish

FOR THE CURRY BASE
4cm piece of fresh ginger,
　peeled
4 garlic cloves
2 red or green chillies
　(or to taste)
1 tsp cumin seeds
4 whole cardamom pods
2 cloves

1 tsp fennel seeds
2 tsp ground cinnamon
2 tsp ground coriander
2–3 tbsp madras curry paste
400g tin chopped tomatoes
salt and ground black pepper

1 Place all the curry base ingredients in a food processor and blitz to form a smooth paste. Season with salt and pepper.

2 Preheat your slow cooker, following the manufacturer's instructions.

3 If your slow cooker has a sauté function, you can use this; if not, use a sauté pan on your hob. Heat the oil, add the lamb and cook until brown. Place in the slow cooker (if you used a separate pan).

4 Add the curry base, onion and peppers to the slow cooker and stir to combine.

5 Set to Low, cover and cook for 8 hours.

6 Sprinkle the curry with the fresh coriander leaves and serve with basmati rice and bread of choice.

A lovely rich casserole, which I like to serve with crusty bread. Aubergine really complements lamb well.

Lamb Ragout with Aubergine

SERVES 4

NUTRITIONAL INFORMATION PER SERVING
348 Kcals
17g fat
13.8g net carbohydrates
3.7g fibre
33g protein

INGREDIENTS
a little coconut oil (optional)
500g stewing lamb, diced
2–3 garlic cloves, chopped
1 red onion, diced
1 aubergine, diced (with skin)
400g tin chopped tomatoes
2 tbsp tomato purée
1 tsp thyme
1 bay leaf
1 tbsp Worcestershire sauce
250ml hot lamb or bone stock
salt and ground black pepper

1 Preheat your slow cooker, following the manufacturer's instructions.

2 Brown the meat first if you like. If your slow cooker has a sauté function, you can use this; if not, use a sauté pan on your hob. Heat a little coconut oil, add the lamb and cook until brown. Place in the slow cooker (if you used a separate pan).

3 Add all the remaining ingredients, combine well and season with salt and pepper.

4 Set to Low, cover and cook for 6–8 hours until the lamb is very tender. Remove the bay leaf.

5 Serve with crusty bread.

This is an economical and very tasty dish. You can marinate the chops in the garlic and herb mixture for 2 hours before slow cooking if you like, though it is not necessary – they are still really flavourful and tender even if they're not marinated. You don't need much liquid as the lamb releases its own juices. I have cooked these without any liquid, but as I am a fan of gravy, I prefer to make it with a bit of extra liquid to spoon over when served, alongside mashed potato and green vegetables.

Braised Lamb Chops

SERVES 4

NUTRITIONAL INFORMATION
PER SERVING
258 Kcals
19g fat
6.6g net carbohydrates
1.9g fibre
15g protein

INGREDIENTS
2 tsp thyme
1 tsp oregano
1 tsp mint
3 garlic cloves, sliced or
  crushed
8 lamb chops
2 large onions, sliced
150ml hot lamb stock
2–3 tsp cornflour (optional)
salt and ground black pepper

1 Preheat your slow cooker, following the manufacturer's instructions.

2 Combine the herbs and garlic in a bowl and season with salt and pepper. Rub the lamb chops with the herb mixture.

3 Place the sliced onions in the base of the slow cooker. Add the lamb stock followed by the seasoned lamb chops.

4 Set to Low, cover and cook for 5–6 hours until the chops are tender.

5 Remove the lamb chops. You can use some of the stock to make a gravy if you wish. To make a gravy, simply mix the cornflour with a little water to make a paste. Add to the stock and place in a pan on the hob over a low–medium heat. Stir until the stock has thickened.

6 Serve with mashed potato and green vegetables.

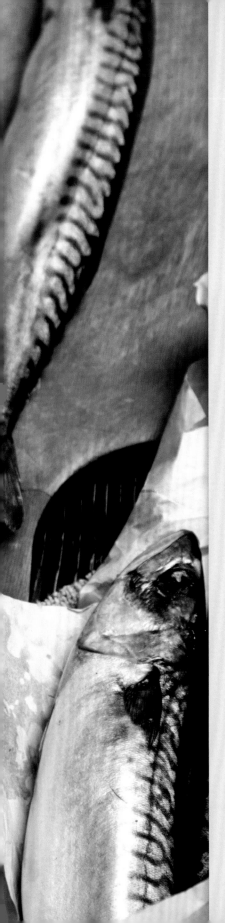

Fish

Fish is normally cooked fast, so you may wonder why you would want to use a slow cooker. You'll be surprised at what you can do with it and how good fish can taste when cooked this way – slow cooking can really enhance its flavour. Slow-cooking fish also traps the odours so that your kitchen doesn't smell too fishy. Use the following advice as a guide and feel free to adapt the recipes in this chapter to suit yourself, or try something new. Speak to your fishmonger to discuss the right type of fish for the slow cooker.

Cooking times

Fish does not need the long cooking time that meat needs. When cooking fish you are looking at a maximum of 3–4 hours and the dish should be eaten straight away as it will dry out if left on the Warm setting. If you want to prepare a meal that will sit in your slow cooker all day when you are at work, fish recipes might not be for you.

Poaching

Poaching fish only takes about 45 minutes on High setting. Add your fish to the stock pot with stock or water and simply poach with a few herbs to add flavour.

Shellfish

If you like shellfish such as prawns, add them to the slow cooker towards the end of the cooking time otherwise they may spoil. If cooking on High, add them in the last 20 minutes. If you are using frozen shellfish, make sure they are completely defrosted before adding them to the stock pot.

This mouth-watering curry works well in the slow cooker, but you do have to watch the timings as ingredients need to be added at different stages. Serve with jasmine rice.

Thai Salmon and Prawn Curry

SERVES 4

NUTRITIONAL INFORMATION
PER SERVING
620 Kcals
42g fat
11g net carbohydrates
2.6g fibre
48g protein

INGREDIENTS
1 tsp olive oil or coconut oil
1 red onion, finely chopped
1–2 garlic cloves, roughly
  chopped
1 lemongrass stalk, tender
  layers finely chopped
4 spring onions, cut into
  4–6cm lengths, including
  green tops
2cm piece of fresh ginger,
  peeled and finely chopped
grated zest and juice of ½ lime
4 tbsp Thai curry paste
400ml tin coconut milk
600g salmon fillets, skinned
  and quartered
100g green beans, cut into
  3–4cm lengths
300g raw shelled prawns,
  deveined
60g baby leaf spinach
salt and ground black pepper

1 Preheat your slow cooker, following the manufacturer's instructions.

2 If your slow cooker has a sauté function, you can use this; if not, use a sauté pan on your hob. Heat the oil over a medium heat, add the red onion and cook for 3–4 minutes until softened, then add the garlic, lemongrass, spring onions and ginger and stir to combine. Place the mixture in the slow cooker (if you used a separate pan).

3 Add all the remaining ingredients apart from the prawns and spinach. Season with salt and pepper.

4 Set to High, cover and cook for 1–1½ hours, until the salmon is cooked to your taste (timings depend on the size and thickness of your salmon).

5 Remove the lid, add the prawns and spinach and continue to cook on High for 20 minutes before serving.

6 Serve with jasmine rice.

This makes a lovely light lunch or simple dinner, served with a green salad and minty new potatoes.

Salmon and Camembert Frittata

SERVES 6

NUTRITIONAL INFORMATION
PER SERVING
437 Kcals
37g fat
2.5g net carbohydrates
0g fibre
24g protein

INGREDIENTS
butter or olive oil, for greasing
1 onion, finely chopped
2 skinless salmon fillets
   (about 250g), chopped
grated zest of ½ lemon
   (and juice, to taste)
200g Camembert, sliced
6 eggs
200ml double cream
a few sprigs of fresh dill,
   finely chopped
black pepper

1 Preheat your slow cooker, following the manufacturer's instructions.

2 Ensure the slow cooker is well greased with butter or olive oil, so you can easily remove the frittata. Alternatively, line the slow cooker with a cake liner or baking parchment.

3 Place the onion and salmon in the base of the slow cooker. Squeeze some lemon juice over the salmon to taste.

4 Add the Camembert slices.

5 Beat the eggs and cream together in a bowl and season with the dill and some black pepper. Pour this over the Camembert – it will soak through, ensuring the whole salmon is covered.

6 Set to High, cover and cook for 1–2 hours.

7 When cooked, remove the stock pot from the cooker base. Run a sharp knife around the edge to help loosen the frittata. If you are using a liner, you should be able to simply lift this out. Alternatively, place a plate on the pot and turn the frittata out onto a plate.

8 Serve hot or cold with salad.

This is my version of this classic chowder. I have added paprika as I think the smokiness it provides goes so well with the clams. This recipe belongs in the fish chapter because it is more of a chunky stew than a soup.

Manhattan Clam Chowder

SERVES 6

NUTRITIONAL INFORMATION
PER SERVING
386 Kcals
23g fat
17g net carbohydrates
4.6g fibre
24g protein

INGREDIENTS
2 tsp olive oil or coconut oil
200g thick diced smoked
 pancetta or lardons
1 large onion, finely chopped
1 garlic clove, crushed
1 red pepper, deseeded and
 roughly diced
2 celery sticks, diced
1 large carrot, diced
400g tin chopped tomatoes
2 tbsp sun-dried tomato paste
 or tomato purée
1 potato, peeled and diced
 into small cubes
2 tsp thyme
1 tsp oregano
¼ tsp cayenne pepper
2 tsp sweet smoked paprika
2 tsp Worcestershire sauce
3–4 dashes of Tabasco sauce
 (to taste)
400ml hot fish stock or
 white wine

1 bay leaf
300g clams, cleaned
 (use mussels if you prefer)
300g raw shelled prawns,
 deveined
a handful of fresh parsley
 leaves, finely chopped
salt and ground black pepper

1 Preheat your slow cooker, following the manufacturer's instructions.

2 If your slow cooker has a sauté function, you can use this; if not, use a sauté pan on your hob. Heat the olive oil or coconut oil, add the bacon and cook for 5 minutes, then add the onion, garlic and red pepper and cook for another 2 minutes. Place in the slow cooker (if you used a separate pan).

3 Add all the remaining ingredients, except the clams, prawns and parsley. Season with salt and pepper.

4 Set to High, cover and cook for 2½–3 hours, or set to Low and cook for 5–6 hours.

5 Half an hour before the end of the cooking time, remove the lid, add the clams and prawns, set to High, cover and cook for 20–30 minutes until they are cooked. Discard any unopened clams and the bay leaf.

6 Serve garnished with the chopped parsley.

This is a simple dish; no herbs or thrills, just plain trout cooked in your slow cooker. Adding a few slices of lemon in the base of the cooker gives the fish a lovely subtle lemon flavour. The cooking time depends on the size of the trout. Serve with a green salad and vinaigrette dressing.

Slow-cooked Trout

SERVES 2

NUTRITIONAL INFORMATION
PER SERVING
344 Kcals
14.3g fat
0g net carbohydrates
0g fibre
54g protein

INGREDIENTS
2 whole rainbow trout, scaled
   and gutted, heads and tails
   removed (or leave them on
   if you wish)
2 lemons, sliced
salt and ground black pepper

1 Preheat your slow cooker, following the manufacturer's instructions. If you are using an older style of slow cooker, place a trivet into the base of the cooker (see page 3).

2 Add 500ml warm water to the slow cooker.

3 Add the sliced lemons, lay the trout over the lemons and season with salt and pepper.

4 Set to High, cover and cook for 45 minutes–1½ hours, depending on the size of your trout, until it's cooked through.

The basic translation of this Brazilian dish is 'fish stew' but doesn't the Brazilian title sound so much better! This is a traditional-style stew, made with creamy coconut and lime. You can use any fish to suit your tastes, but for this recipe I have kept it simple and used cod fillets. Serve with basmati rice.

Moqueca de Peixe

SERVES 4

NUTRITIONAL INFORMATION
PER SERVING
769 Kcals
57g fat
17g net carbohydrates
4.3g fibre
43g protein

INGREDIENTS
2 tsp coconut oil
1 large onion, finely chopped
1 green pepper, deseeded and
  sliced
1 red pepper, deseeded and
  sliced
4 garlic cloves, crushed
2 red chillies, thinly sliced
400ml tin coconut milk
200g block of coconut cream,
  chopped
3 tomatoes, sliced
grated zest and juice of 3 limes
500g skinless cod fillets,
  halved or quartered
350g raw shelled prawns,
  deveined
a large handful of chopped
  fresh coriander, plus extra
  to garnish
salt and ground black pepper

1 Preheat your slow cooker, following the manufacturer's instructions.

2 If your slow cooker has a sauté function, you can use this; if not, use a sauté pan on your hob. Heat the coconut oil, add the onion, peppers, garlic and chillies and cook for 2 minutes until softened. Place in the slow cooker (if you used a separate pan).

3 Add all the remaining ingredients to the slow cooker, except the prawns and coriander. Season with salt and pepper.

4 Set to High, cover and cook for 1–2 hours, or set to Low and cook for 3–4 hours. The cooking time will depend on the size of your fish fillets.

5 Half an hour before the end of the cooking time, remove the lid, add the prawns and coriander, set to High, cover and cook for another 30 minutes, until the prawns are cooked through.

6 Garnish with coriander and serve with basmati rice.

There really is nothing nicer than salmon baked in foil, served with a variety of salad leaves. This recipe is very basic, retaining the delicate flavour of the salmon. All the salmon is adorned with is a little olive oil, seasoning and lemon, but feel free to add herbs to suit your own taste.

Salmon Parcels

SERVES 4

NUTRITIONAL INFORMATION
PER SERVING
288 Kcals
19g fat
1g net carbohydrates
0.4g fibre
28g protein

INGREDIENTS
4 salmon fillets
 (about 125g each)
1 lemon, sliced
1–2 tbsp olive oil
salt and ground black pepper

1 Preheat your slow cooker, following the manufacturer's instructions.

2 Place 1 large or 4 smaller squares of foil on your worktop (depending on whether you want to cook the salmon all in one parcel or individually).

3 Place a slice of lemon in the centre of each piece of foil (or most of the lemon slices on one larger sheet of foil). Add the salmon fillets and top each fillet with another slice of lemon. Season well with salt and pepper and add a small drizzle of olive oil (about 1 teaspoon of oil per fillet).

4 Wrap the foil securely around the fish and place the parcel in the base of the slow cooker.

5 Set to Low, cover and cook for 2–3 hours, until the salmon is cooked to your liking. The cooking time will depend on the size and thickness of your salmon fillets.

6 Be careful when removing the salmon as the foil gets very hot.

7 Serve with a variety of salad leaves.

Vegetarian and Vegan

The recipes in this chapter are

suitable for vegans and vegetarians but don't assume they aren't useful if you eat meat. These recipes are all delicious and suitable for everyone. Each one is a scrumptious family favourite packed with flavour.

Vegan and plant-based diets are growing in popularity. Some people have adopted this way of eating 100 per cent; others are opting to eat less meat and try to have one or two days a week when they are vegan or vegetarian. If you are vegan, it is important to ensure you have enough nutrients in your diet, particularly good-quality proteins, healthy fats, minerals, iron and vitamins (especially B12).

The slow cooker works well for both vegan and vegetarian dishes. Here's a selection of my personal favourites.

This is a lovely curry made from potato and aubergine. If you want to increase the protein content of the curry, add a tin of chickpeas. You can also add some spinach for extra nutrients and flavour.

Aloo Baingan

SERVES 4
VG

NUTRITIONAL INFORMATION
PER SERVING
306 Kcals
7.9g fat
45g net carbohydrates
9.9g fibre
7.4g protein

INGREDIENTS
2 tsp coconut oil
1 tsp cumin seeds
1 tsp mustard seeds
1 tsp coriander seeds
2–3 tbsp curry paste (I use
  Massaman curry paste)
1–2 red or green chillies
  (to taste)
3cm piece of fresh ginger,
  peeled
3 garlic cloves
3 tomatoes
200ml coconut milk
1 large onion, chopped
2 large potatoes, peeled and
  thickly diced or cut into
  wedges
2 aubergines, thickly sliced
  or diced
2–3 curry leaves
salt and ground black pepper

1 Preheat your slow cooker following the manufacturer's instructions.

2 If your slow cooker has a sauté function, you can use this; if not, use a sauté pan on your hob. Heat the coconut oil, add the spice seeds and fry for 2 minutes until fragrant, then place in a food processor.

3 Add the curry paste, chilli, ginger, garlic, tomatoes and coconut milk to the food processor and blitz until smooth. Season with salt and pepper.

4 Place the onion, potato, aubergine and curry leaves in the slow cooker and pour over the spicy sauce.

5 Set to Low, cover and cook for 6–8 hours. Serve with basmati rice and naan bread.

I love frittatas. They are so versatile and are ideal for using up the leftovers in your fridge. They make great breakfast, lunch and picnic meals, and, thanks to the high egg content, are packed with nutrients such as protein.

Broccoli, Onion and Feta Frittata

SERVES 6

NUTRITIONAL INFORMATION
PER SERVING
357 Kcals
32g fat
4.1g net carbohydrates
1.5g fibre
12g protein

INGREDIENTS
butter or olive oil, for greasing
1 onion, finely chopped
150g broccoli florets, chopped
110g feta cheese, crumbled
6 eggs
200ml double cream
salt and ground black pepper

1 Preheat your slow cooker, following the manufacturer's instructions.

2 Ensure the slow cooker is well greased with butter or olive oil, so you can easily remove the frittata. Alternatively, line the slow cooker with a cake liner or baking parchment.

3 Layer the vegetables and cheese in the slow cooker, ensuring they are evenly distributed.

4 Beat the eggs and cream together in a bowl and season with salt and pepper. Pour this over the vegetables and cheese – the mixture will soak through, ensuring the whole thing is covered.

5 Set to High, cover and cook for 1–2 hours.

6 When cooked, remove the stock pot from the cooker base. Run a sharp knife around the edge to help loosen the frittata. Carefully place a plate over the pot, then turn the pot and plate over so the frittata drops onto the plate.

7 Serve hot or cold with salad.

Jackfruit is the new wonder fruit that is transforming vegan food. Jackfruit is a very large fruit that, when ripe, has a tropical taste, but it's the unripe, green jackfruit that's used in cooking. It does not really taste of much when unripe, so is great for absorbing flavours. It is very fibrous so when it's cooked and 'pulled' apart it has the look and texture of pulled pork. You can buy jackfruit in the UK in tins, ready to use. I like to serve this in toasted buns with coleslaw or avocado, lettuce and tomato.

Jackfruit 'Pulled Pork'

SERVES 6
VG

NUTRITIONAL INFORMATION
PER SERVING
186 Kcals
0.7g fat
41g net carbohydrates
2.4g fibre
2.2g protein

INGREDIENTS
2 x 400g tins jackfruit in
  water, drained
1 red onion, finely chopped
2 garlic cloves, crushed
1–2 red or green chillies, finely
  chopped (to taste)
1 tbsp apple cider vinegar
3 tsp smoked paprika
2 tsp oregano
2 tsp Tabasco sauce
1 tsp ground cumin
1 tsp ground cinnamon
400g tin chopped tomatoes
4 tbsp barbecue sauce
100ml hot vegetable stock
salt and ground black pepper

1 Preheat your slow cooker, following the manufacturer's instructions.

2 Place all the ingredients in the slow cooker, season with salt and pepper and combine well.

3 Set to Low, cover and cook for 4–5 hours.

4 Half an hour before the end of the cooking time, remove the lid and use a fork to shred the jackfruit to create a 'pulled pork' effect.

5 Cover and cook on Low for another 20–30 minutes.

6 Serve in toasted buns with coleslaw or slices of avocado, lettuce and tomato.

This is so easy to make and costs very little. My version is mild and creamy, but you can make it spicier by adding a few chopped chillies.

Creamy Masoor Dhal

SERVES 4

 VG

NUTRITIONAL INFORMATION
PER SERVING
288 Kcals
11g fat
30g net carbohydrates
6.2g fibre
12g protein

INGREDIENTS
2 tsp coconut oil or olive oil
1 onion, finely chopped
2 garlic cloves, crushed
3cm piece of fresh ginger,
  peeled and finely chopped
1 red pepper, deseeded and
  finely chopped
2–3 tbsp mild curry powder
  (to taste)
1 tsp ground turmeric
3 tomatoes, finely chopped
150g red lentils, rinsed
1 tbsp tomato purée
400ml tin coconut milk
3 tbsp coconut cream
salt and ground black pepper
2 tbsp desiccated coconut,
  to serve

1 Preheat your slow cooker, following the manufacturer's instructions.

2 Place all the ingredients, except the desiccated coconut, in the slow cooker and stir well until combined. Season well with salt and pepper.

3 Set to Low, cover and cook for 6–8 hours.

4 Sprinkle with desiccated coconut and serve with chapatis, parathas or naan bread.

This protein-rich variation of a ratatouille includes mixed beans. You don't have to add the beans, but they provide more nutrients and turn it into a lovely, complete meal. Serve the ratatouille with basmati rice, spiralised courgette or cauliflower rice, if you like.

Loaded Ratatouille

SERVES 6

NUTRITIONAL INFORMATION PER SERVING
368 Kcals
23g fat
13.4g net carbohydrates
6.4g fibre
24g protein

INGREDIENTS
2 red onions, sliced
2–3 garlic cloves, roughly chopped
1 red pepper, deseeded and roughly diced
1 yellow pepper, deseeded and roughly diced
2 courgettes, roughly diced
1–2 aubergines, roughly diced
6 tomatoes, roughly diced (or 400g tin chopped tomatoes)
400g tin mixed beans, drained
175ml hot vegetable stock
2 tbsp sun-dried tomato paste or tomato purée
1 tsp oregano
1 tsp parsley
½ tsp paprika
salt and ground black pepper

1 Preheat your slow cooker, following the manufacturer's instructions.

2 Place all the ingredients in the slow cooker. Season with salt and pepper.

3 Set to High, cover and cook for 3 hours, or set to Low and cook for 5–6 hours – be careful not to overcook it, as there is nothing worse than a slimy ratatouille.

4 Serve the ratatouille with rice, spiralised courgette or cauliflower rice.

This recipe is stupidly easy: just add all the ingredients to the pot and walk away. Even our grumpy teenager could manage this! I use nutritional yeast flakes in this recipe – they are great for adding a cheesy flavour to the dish, as well as adding nutrients. When buying cheese, check the label to ensure it is suitable for vegetarians.

Ridiculously Easy Macaroni Cheese

SERVES 4

NUTRITIONAL INFORMATION PER SERVING
463 Kcals
25g fat
33g net carbohydrates
2.2g fibre
25g protein

INGREDIENTS
1 litre full-fat milk
250g mature Cheddar, grated
125g cream cheese
40g Italian hard cheese, grated
1–2 tbsp nutritional yeast
    flakes (optional)
½ tsp English mustard powder
    (optional)
400g dried macaroni
salt and ground black pepper

1 Preheat your slow cooker, following the manufacturer's instructions.

2 Place all the ingredients into the slow cooker, stir to combine, and season with salt and pepper.

3 Set to Low, cover and cook for 2 hours, or until the pasta is cooked.

4 Serve immediately.

This very creamy vegetable, fruit and nut korma is delicious when served with basmati rice or, for a lower carb option, cauliflower rice. Add 250g cubed paneer or tofu if you want to increase the protein content, adding them for the last 30 minutes of cooking with your slow cooker set to High.

Navratan Korma

SERVES 6

 VG

NUTRITIONAL INFORMATION
PER SERVING
488 Kcals
31g fat
39g net carbohydrates
6.8g fibre
8.5g protein

INGREDIENTS
1 large onion, diced
1 yellow pepper, deseeded
  and diced
1 carrot, diced
1 potato, peeled and diced
1 sweet potato, peeled and
  diced
1 small cauliflower, broken
  into florets
2–3 slices of pineapple, diced
  (tinned or fresh)
200g coconut cream
250ml coconut milk
50g sultanas
60g unsalted cashew nuts
salt and ground black pepper

FOR THE KORMA PASTE
2 garlic cloves
2–3cm piece of fresh ginger,
  peeled
2–3 tbsp korma curry powder
  (to taste)
½ tsp ground cumin
1 tsp ground turmeric
¼ tsp ground or freshly
  grated nutmeg
1–2 red or green chillies
  (to taste)
2–3 tomatoes

1 Place all the korma paste ingredients in a food processor and blitz to form a paste. Season with salt and pepper.

2 Make sure all the pieces of vegetables are roughly the same size.

3 Preheat your slow cooker, following the manufacturer's instructions.

4 Place the vegetables and pineapple in the slow cooker. Pour in the korma paste and add the coconut cream, coconut milk, sultanas and cashews.

5 Set to Low, cover and cook for 6–8 hours.

6 Serve with basmati or cauliflower rice.

You can use any beans for this chilli, or even a combination of beans. Just like any chilli, the flavour improves over a day or two. Double up the recipe and freeze to make quick-and-easy ready meals for those busy weekday evenings. Serve it with brown basmati rice or, for a lower carb option, cauliflower rice, and sour cream on the side. For added colour, top with grated cheese, sliced green chilli and chopped spring onions.

Vegetable and Bean Chilli

SERVES 4

 VG

NUTRITIONAL INFORMATION
PER SERVING
382 Kcals
13g fat
43g net carbohydrates
8.5g fibre
17g protein

INGREDIENTS
1 tsp coconut oil
1 large red onion, chopped
2 star anise
2 garlic cloves, crushed
1–2 red or green chillies
   (to taste), finely chopped
1 red pepper, deseeded
   and diced
1 carrot, finely diced
1 celery stick, diced
1–2 tsp chilli powder
   (or to taste)
2 tsp smoked paprika
¼ tsp cayenne pepper
1 tsp marjoram
2 tsp oregano
400g tin chopped tomatoes
2 tbsp sun-dried tomato paste
400g tin black-eyed beans,
   drained
400g tin red kidney beans,
   drained
75g red lentils, rinsed
350ml hot water or vegetable
   stock
salt and ground black pepper

1 Preheat the slow cooker, following the manufacturer's instructions.

2 If your slow cooker has a sauté function, you can use this; if not, use a sauté pan on your hob over a medium heat. Heat the oil, add the onion, star anise, garlic, chilli and red pepper and sauté gently until they start to soften slightly. Add the carrot and celery, then all the spices and herbs. Cook for a further minute, then remove and discard the star anise and place the contents of the pan in the slow cooker (if you used a separate pan). Add all the remaining ingredients and combine well. Season with salt and pepper.

3 Set to Low, cover and cook for 6–8 hours.

4 Serve with brown basmati rice, or cauliflower rice, with some sour cream.

This is not only a great vegan dish, it is also a lovely side dish to have with other curries, and is particularly good for dinner parties. You can prepare most curries at least one day in advance, as they do generally improve with age, and then just reheat to serve. Serve with basmati rice, cauliflower rice or flatbreads.

Tofu Tikka Masala

SERVES 4
VG

NUTRITIONAL INFORMATION PER SERVING
657 Kcals
54g fat
19g net carbohydrates
6.2g fibre
19g protein

INGREDIENTS
60g unsalted cashew nuts
2 garlic cloves
2 red or green chillies
4 whole cardamom pods
2 tsp ground cinnamon
4 coriander seeds
1 tbsp tikka masala curry powder (or to taste)
2 tbsp smooth almond butter
2 tomatoes, quartered
1 tbsp tomato purée
200g block coconut cream, softened according to the packet instructions
1 large onion, chopped
1 red pepper, deseeded and sliced
400g tofu, cut into thick chunks
a small handful of fresh coriander

1 Soak the cashews in a bowl of 200ml cold water for 30 minutes.

2 Place the soaked cashews, along with the liquid, in a food processor. Add the garlic, chillies, cardamom, cinnamon, coriander seeds, curry powder, almond butter, tomatoes, tomato purée and coconut cream and blitz until smooth.

3 Preheat your slow cooker, following the manufacturer's instructions.

4 Place the onion, red pepper and tofu in the slow cooker and add the mixture from the food processor.

5 Set to Low, cover and cook for 4–6 hours. Just before serving, remove the lid and stir in most of the fresh coriander leaves.

6 Serve the curry garnished with the remaining coriander.

Desserts

We don't often think of making

desserts in the slow cooker, but your versatile machine will surprise you with the sheer variety of delicious sweet dishes it can create. I love my slow cooker so much I've even bought a small slow cooker that I only use for desserts.

Cakes and sponges

Cakes and sponges will not have the same light texture as they do when baked in the oven, but they will be just as delicious and popular with your family.

Dietary swaps

As a society, we are becoming increasingly conscious of our health and the way our diets impact upon it. If you're new to gluten-free, vegan and sugar-free baking ingredients, here are my top tips on the best products out there, and advice for converting any recipe into your way of eating.

GLUTEN-FREE We have some fantastic gluten-free flours available now. My favourite is from Doves Farm. You can swap like-for-like and achieve great results, though I have found adding roughly 30ml more liquid when using gluten-free flour in cakes and sponge puddings produces better results. Gluten-free suet is available – always check the label.

VEGAN You can buy vegan margarines that work as a direct swap for butter. You can also use coconut oil. For a dairy milk alternative, switch to almond, coconut or rice milk. You can buy egg replacements, but I make my own by mixing 1 tablespoon of flax or chia seeds with an equal amount of water, leaving it to soak for 30 minutes then using this as a binder weight for weight for every egg in a recipe. You can also use nut butters, stewed fruit or mashed banana as a binder. Cashews are very good for vegan cooking as they can be soaked to form a creamy base – ideal for desserts and even soups. Vegetarian suet is usually suitable for vegans.

SUGAR-FREE Cutting sugar from the diet is a particular passion of mine – I have written several books on sugar-free diets. Sugar is easily swapped: simply use erythritol or xylitol instead, both of which look and taste like sugar but have very little impact on your blood sugars and insulin levels. You can also use Stevia in granulated or liquid form, but this is over 300 times sweeter than sugar, so it can be hard to gauge how much to use. If you are reducing your sugar consumption, remember that natural foods such as bananas, dates, dried fruit, fruit juices, honey, maple syrup etc., are all packed with glucose and fructose, so this is only a sideways step. If you're looking to keep your sugar intake low, you will need to cut these down or avoid them entirely.

How to get a pudding bowl in and out of the slow cooker

Puddings are great when made in a slow cooker, but it can be tricky to get them in and out without burning yourself. To avoid accidents, make yourself a string handle or a foil strap.

STRING HANDLE If I am using string to tie a handle to the top of a basin, I cut a second piece, around 40cm long, and double it over, looping it around both sides of the top of the basin and tying in the middle to form a handle.

FOIL STRAP Simply cut a sheet of foil big enough to fit around the pudding bowl and give yourself enough to hold on to. I use a 40–50cm piece for my 1.2-litre bowl. Fold the foil lengthways until you have a strong strap around 5cm wide. Place the bowl in the centre of the strap and fold the excess over the top. Place the bowl in your slow cooker and when you need to remove the dessert, simply unfold the straps and lift it out.

How to stop cakes and sponges getting soggy in a slow cooker

The slow cooker can sometimes get quite wet inside because of the condensation/steam. To prevent this from affecting your cakes or sponges, simply place a tea towel over the top of the slow cooker before adding the lid. Pop on the lid and push down firmly to ensure it forms a good seal (this is not necessary if you are slow-cooking a pudding with a foil or parchment lid).

This recipe brings childhood memories rushing back – this pudding is pure comfort food and is perfect when served with homemade custard, ice cream or crème fraîche.

Cinnamon, Sultana and Apple Steamed Pudding

NUTRITIONAL
INFORMATION PER SERVING
(FOR 8 SERVINGS)
406 Kcals
21g fat
48g net carbohydrates
2.1g fibre
6.1g protein

EQUIPMENT
You will need a 1.2-litre pudding bowl, baking parchment, foil and string (I like to use double-sided parchment from Lakeland, with foil on one side and parchment on the other).

INGREDIENTS
175g butter, softened, plus extra for greasing
150g sugar
3 large eggs
220g self-raising flour
75g sultanas
2 cooking apples, peeled and diced
2 tsp ground cinnamon
nutmeg, for grating

1 Grease the pudding bowl thoroughly and generously with butter and set to one side. You can place a circle of baking parchment at the base of the bowl if you are worried about the pudding sticking.

2 Cream the butter and sugar together in a mixing bowl until light and fluffy. Add the eggs, one at a time, beating well, then sift in the flour.

3 Add the sultanas, apple, cinnamon and a generous grating of nutmeg. Stir well.

4 Place the mixture into your pudding bowl. Cover the pudding bowl with baking parchment, pleating it at the centre to allow for expansion, then add a pleated layer of foil and tie very securely with string. Make a handle with string or foil to make it easier to lift the pudding in and out of the slow cooker (see page 153).

5 Boil the kettle. Place the pudding in the base of your slow cooker. Add boiling water to the slow cooker until it comes halfway up the sides of the pudding bowl.

6 Set to High, cover and cook for 3–4 hours, or set to Low, cover and cook for 6–8 hours, or until the sponge springs back when touched.

7 Remove the pudding from the slow cooker using the handle. Run a knife around the edge of the pudding. Place a plate on the top of the bowl and carefully flip the plate and bowl, to turn out the pudding. Serve warm with accompaniment of choice.

We often think of tapioca pudding as an old-fashioned pudding we were served at school, but I think it deserves a revival as it was always one of my favourites.
I like to use large tapioca pearls, but you can use the standard small pearls if you prefer.

Classic Tapioca Pudding

SERVES 4

NUTRITIONAL INFORMATION
PER SERVING
352 Kcals
10g fat
54g net carbohydrates
0g fibre
10g protein

INGREDIENTS
1 litre full-fat milk
100g sugar
2 tsp vanilla bean extract
   or paste
1 large egg, beaten
75g large tapioca pearls
nutmeg, for grating

1 Preheat your slow cooker, following the manufacturer's instructions.

2 Mix the milk, sugar, vanilla and egg together in a bowl until evenly combined.

3 Stir in the tapioca pearls and pour the mixture into the slow cooker.

4 Set to Low, cover and cook for 4–6 hours, stirring occasionally. The finished pudding should be nice and thick when cooked, but you can add more milk if you don't want it as thick.

5 Serve warm with a sprinkle of grated nutmeg.

Almonds and plums go together well. This is a lovely cake, perfect served as a pudding with a dollop of cream or homemade custard. You can make this in individual ramekins, or bake it as one large cake in your slow cooker.

Almond and Plum Sponge

SERVES 8

NUTRITIONAL INFORMATION
PER SERVING
599 Kcals
38g fat
50g net carbohydrates
4.7g fibre
11g protein

EQUIPMENT
You will need 6–8 ramekins, or if you're cooking it as a large pudding you'll need a large cake liner or baking parchment.

INGREDIENTS
225g butter, softened, plus
   extra for greasing
200g sugar
4 eggs, beaten
135g ground almonds
200g self-raising flour, sifted
½ tsp baking powder
1 tsp almond extract
75ml full-fat milk
5 ripe plums, destoned and
   roughly chopped
35g flaked almonds

1 Line your slow cooker with a cake liner or grease it with butter and line with baking parchment, leaving enough around the edges to help you lift the cake out. Alternatively, make the cakes in greased individual ramekins: these will cook much faster than the large cake (and you will need to cook them in batches if you can't fit them in one layer in your slow cooker).

2 Preheat your slow cooker, following the manufacturer's instructions.

3 Cream the butter and sugar together in a bowl until light and fluffy. Add the eggs one at a time, beat well, then add the ground almonds, flour and baking powder and fold in. Add the almond extract and milk and combine well.

4 Add the roughly chopped plums and fold them into the cake mixture.

5 Pour the mixture into your slow cooker and level out the surface. Sprinkle with the flaked almonds.

6 Cover your slow cooker with a tea towel before placing on the lid firmly, ensuring it is well secured.

7 Set to High and cook for 1½–2 hours. Test if it's done by inserting a skewer into the centre – if it comes out clean, the sponge is cooked. Remember that individual ramekin dishes will need less cooking so check them after 1 hour.

8 Lift the cake out of the slow cooker. Serve hot or cold with a dollop of clotted cream.

This is a very indulgent sweet pudding but we all need a treat once in a while! You can use any dates, but personally I feel that medjool dates give the best flavour and sweetness. This really doesn't need to be served with anything other than the sauce topping, but if you want to add to the indulgence, you can add a dollop of clotted cream.

Sticky Toffee Pudding

SERVES 8

NUTRITIONAL INFORMATION PER SERVING
555 Kcals
30g fat
65g net carbohydrates
2.9g fibre
5.5g protein

EQUIPMENT
You will need a 1.2-litre pudding bowl, baking parchment, foil and string. (I like to use double-sided parchment from Lakeland, with foil on one side and parchment on the other).

INGREDIENTS
225g medjool dates, pitted and chopped
300ml double cream
200g brown sugar
5 tsp black treacle
75g butter, softened, plus extra for greasing
2 large eggs
1 tsp vanilla extract or paste
200g self-raising flour
1 tsp bicarbonate of soda

1 Grease the pudding bowl thoroughly and generously with butter and set to one side.

2 Place the chopped dates and 300ml water in a pan, bring to the boil and simmer for 2 minutes, then remove from the heat. Set to one side and leave to soak for at least 20 minutes.

3 Place the cream, sugar and 3 teaspoons of the treacle in a pan over a medium-low heat and stir until the sugar has dissolved. Simmer gently for 2 minutes then remove from the heat. Set to one side.

4 Cream the butter and sugar together in a bowl until light and fluffy. Add the eggs, vanilla and remaining 2 teaspoons of treacle, beat well then combine the flour and bicarbonate of soda and sift them into the mixture.

5 Add the dates, including their soaking liquid, and combine well.

6 Pour half the cream mixture into the base of the pudding bowl (reserving the rest for drizzling over the finished pudding).

7 Place the mixture into your pudding bowl. Cover the pudding bowl with baking parchment, pleating it at the centre to allow for expansion, then add a pleated layer of foil and tie very securely with string. Make a handle with string or foil to make it easier to lift the pudding in and out of the slow cooker (see page 153).

8 Boil the kettle. Place the pudding in the base of your slow cooker. Add boiling water to the slow cooker until it comes halfway up the sides of the pudding bowl.

9 Set to High, cover and cook for 3–4 hours, or set to Low, cover and cook for 6–8 hours, or until the sponge springs back when touched.

10 Remove from the slow cooker. Gently heat the remaining creamy toffee sauce.

11 Run a knife around the edge of the pudding. Place a plate on the top of the bowl and carefully flip the plate and the bowl, to turn out the pudding.

12 Serve immediately with the remaining toffee sauce.

I get cravings for milky pudding whenever I am feeling under the weather. Rice pudding is incredibly comforting. I love to add cinnamon to my rice pudding, but you can omit this if you prefer. For a different flavour, why not try adding the seeds from 8 crushed cardamom pods along with the sugar, and using coconut cream instead of double cream? If you are vegan, you could swap the milk for coconut milk and add a 200ml carton of vegan cream to create a creamy consistency and flavour.

Traditional Rice Pudding

SERVES 6

NUTRITIONAL INFORMATION
PER SERVING
374 Kcals
26g fat
27g net carbohydrates
0g fibre
7.1g protein

INGREDIENTS
1 litre full-fat milk
3 tbsp sugar (or to taste)
80g pudding rice
1 cinnamon stick
1 tbsp butter, plus extra
   for greasing
200ml double cream
nutmeg, for grating

1 Grease the slow cooker bowl with butter.

2 Preheat your slow cooker, following the manufacturer's instructions.

3 Place the milk, sugar, rice and cinnamon stick in the slow cooker then dot with the butter.

4 Set to Low, cover and cook for 5–6 hours, stirring every now and again, otherwise the rice may stick or cook in lumps.

5 Once cooked, remove the lid and discard the cinnamon stick. Add the cream and stir until combined. Set to High, cover and cook for a further 15 minutes, stirring occasionally. Add more milk if needed until you get the consistency you desire.

6 Serve the hot rice pudding with a grating of nutmeg.

Who doesn't love chocolate cheesecake? This is gorgeous, made with good-quality dark chocolate and some orange extract. If you don't want the orange flavour, you can omit this, but I have always been mad for chocolate orange.

Baked Chocolate Orange Cheesecake

SERVES 8

NUTRITIONAL INFORMATION
PER SERVING
463 Kcals
35g fat
23g net carbohydrates
3.4g fibre
13g protein

EQUIPMENT
You will need 8 ramekins,
or if you're cooking it as a
large cheesecake you'll need
a large cake liner or baking
parchment.

INGREDIENTS
200g digestive biscuits
50g butter, melted, plus extra
  for greasing if needed
20g cocoa powder
3 eggs, separated
500g cream cheese
200g sour cream
grated zest of 1 orange
1 tsp orange extract
100g good-quality dark
  chocolate (min 70% cocoa
  solids), melted, plus
  30g dark chocolate shavings,
  to garnish

1 Line your slow cooker with a cake liner or grease it with butter and line with baking parchment (or grease the ramekins).

2 Preheat your slow cooker, following the manufacturer's instructions.

3 Crush the biscuits until they form fine crumbs and combine in a bowl with the cocoa powder. Add the melted butter and stir well.

4 Press the biscuit mixture into the ramekins or lined base of your slow cooker.

5 Mix the egg yolks in a bowl with the cream cheese, sour cream, orange zest and orange extract.

6 Beat the egg whites in a separate, clean bowl until they form soft peaks. Fold the egg whites into the cream cheese mixture, then fold in the melted dark chocolate.

7 Place the mixture into your ramekins or lined base in your slow cooker (if you can't fit the ramekins in one layer in your slow cooker you will need to cook them in batches).

8 If you are using ramekin dishes, place them in the slow cooker and pour in boiling water until it comes around halfway up the ramekins. If you are placing the mixture directly into the slow cooker, you do not need to do this.

9 Cover your slow cooker with a tea towel before placing on the lid firmly, ensuring it is well secured.

10 Set to Low and cook for 2–2½ hours until firm.

11 Remove the cheesecake from the slow cooker and leave to cool. Once cool, place in the fridge to chill for at least 3 hours or overnight.

12 When ready to serve, garnish with chocolate shavings.

TOP TIP
If your slow cooker is large enough, you may be able to get a cake tin inside. If not, you can use a large cake liner or grease your slow cooker well and line it with baking parchment (you will not be adding hot water to your slow cooker!). You can also use individual ramekins – if this is the case, you will need to reduce the cooking time by half.

This is one of my favourite desserts. This recipe is for a traditional vanilla crème brûlée, but you can add other flavours or some berries if you like. I would recommend making the brûlée topping with a blowtorch but if you don't have one, you could use a hot grill.

Crème Brûlée

SERVES 4

NUTRITIONAL INFORMATION
PER SERVING
490 Kcals
44g fat
19g net carbohydrates
0g fibre
3.4g protein

EQUIPMENT
You will need 4 ramekins.

INGREDIENTS
300ml double cream
1 tsp good-quality vanilla
  bean paste
3 egg yolks
40g sugar
30g brown sugar, for topping

1 Preheat your slow cooker, following the manufacturer's instructions.

2 Pour the double cream into a saucepan, add the vanilla bean paste and bring to a simmer. Remove from the heat as soon as it reaches simmering point.

3 Beat the eggs yolks and sugar together in a bowl until pale in colour. Gradually add the warm cream to the egg mixture, stirring continuously with a balloon whisk until it is mixed in thoroughly. Pour the mixture into your ramekins.

4 If you are using an older style of slow cooker, place a trivet into the base of the cooker (see page 3). Place the ramekins in the slow cooker and pour boiling water into the slow cooker until it reaches halfway up the ramekins.

5 Set to High, cover and cook for 1–1½ hours, until the custards are set.

6 Remove from the slow cooker and leave to cool, then place in the fridge and chill for at least 3 hours.

7 When ready to serve, sprinkle the brown sugar evenly over the crème brûlées. Using your kitchen blowtorch or a hot grill, heat the sugar until it changes to a golden colour. If you are using the grill, be careful and watch it as the sugar can burn very quickly. Serve immediately.

TOP TIP
Don't throw away the egg whites. Freeze them for making into a lovely meringue.

Blackberry and pear are a lovely combination, coming together here to make a delicious pudding that's perfect served with homemade custard. You can swap the pears for Bramley cooking apples if you prefer.

Blackberry and Pear Upside-down Cake

SERVES 6–8

NUTRITIONAL INFORMATION
PER SERVING
(FOR 8 SERVINGS)
420 Kcals
23g fat
47g net carbohydrates
2.6g fibre
5.3g protein

EQUIPMENT
You will need 6–8 ramekins, or if you're cooking it as a large cake you'll need a large cake liner or baking parchment.

INGREDIENTS
200g butter, softened, plus
  extra for greasing
150g sugar
3 eggs
1 tsp vanilla extract
180g self-raising flour, sifted
50g brown sugar
2–3 pears, peeled, cored and
  sliced lengthways (you can
  use tinned)
75g blackberries

1 Line your slow cooker with a cake liner or grease it with butter and line with baking parchment, leaving enough around the edges to help you lift out the cake. Alternatively, grease your ramekin dishes, ensuring they are very well greased.

2 Cream 150g of the butter with the sugar in a bowl and beat until light and fluffy. Add the eggs one by one, beating well between each addition, then add the vanilla extract. Fold in the sifted flour until combined.

3 Heat the remaining 50g butter with the brown sugar over a low heat until dissolved.

4 Place the sliced pears and blackberries in your ramekins or the lined base of your slow cooker. Pour over the butter/brown sugar syrup.

5 Top the fruit with the cake batter and smooth it out.

6 If you are using ramekins, place them in the slow cooker and pour in boiling water until it comes halfway up the sides of the ramekins (if you can't fit them in one layer in your slow cooker you will need to cook them in batches). If you are placing the mixture directly into the slow cooker, you do not need to do this.

7 Cover your slow cooker with a tea towel before placing on the lid firmly, ensuring it is well secured.

8 Set to Low and cook for 3–3½ hours, or until the cake is firm to touch.

9 Carefully remove the cake from the slow cooker, taking care not to burn yourself.

10 Flip the cake over onto a plate so the pear and blackberry base is at the top.

11 Serve hot with homemade custard.

TOP TIP

If your slow cooker is large enough, you may be able to get a cake tin inside. If not, you can use a large cake liner or grease your slow cooker well and line it with baking parchment (but you will not be adding hot water to your slow cooker!). You can also use individual ramekins – if this is the case, you will need to reduce the cooking time by half.

I have always been fascinated by self-saucing puddings. We used to have lemon sponge when we were children and I couldn't understand how Mum poured liquid over the top of the cake mix then the sauce appeared underneath when cooked. This is a more grown-up version of a childhood classic. Make sure you use good-quality dark chocolate to get a lovely, rich flavour. Serve with thick cream or crème fraîche and extra black cherries.

Black Forest Self-saucing Chocolate Pudding

SERVES 6

NUTRITIONAL INFORMATION
PER SERVING
592 Kcals
27g fat
65g net carbohydrates
4.3g fibre
9.3g protein

EQUIPMENT
You will need 1 large
ovenproof dish that fits
in your slow cooker, or
4 ramekins.

INGREDIENTS
110g butter, softened, plus
  extra for greasing
100g sugar
2 eggs
1 tsp vanilla bean extract
  or paste
150g self-raising flour
30g cocoa powder
75g dark chocolate, melted
50ml kirsch
100g pitted black cherries
  (tinned or frozen), halved

FOR THE SAUCE
150ml kirsch
75g sugar
50g cocoa powder

1 Preheat your slow cooker, following the manufacturer's instructions.

2 Grease your ovenproof dish or individual ramekins very thoroughly with butter.

3 Cream the butter and sugar together in a mixing bowl until light and fluffy. Add the eggs and vanilla, beat well, then add the sifted flour and cocoa. Combine well.

4 Fold the melted chocolate gently into the sponge batter, followed by the kirsch and black cherries.

5 Pour the batter into the greased ovenproof dish or ramekins.

6 To make the sauce, combine the kirsch, sugar and cocoa powder with 200ml boiling water. Pour this onto the batter.

7 If you are using an older style of slow cooker, place a trivet into the base of the cooker (see page 3). Add the ovenproof dish or ramekins, then pour boiling water into the slow cooker until it reaches halfway up the sides of the ovenproof dish or ramekins.

8 Cover your slow cooker with a tea towel before placing on the lid firmly, ensuring it is well secured.

9 Set to High, and if using ramekins, cook for 1 hour, then check. If using a large ovenproof dish, cook for 1½–2 hours. The pudding should be firm to the touch.

10 Serve immediately with a dollop of cream or crème fraîche and any leftover black cherries.

This is a wonderful alternative to traditional bread and butter pudding. Because brioche is quite buttery, you don't need to add butter to each slice (unless you want to!). You can use panettone, or white bread if you prefer. You can prepare this in your slow cooker base or place an ovenproof dish inside the slow cooker. If your slow cooker doesn't have a non-stick pot, I would opt for the latter.

Cranberry and Orange Brioche and Butter Pudding

SERVES 6

NUTRITIONAL INFORMATION
PER SERVING
326 Kcals
9.1g fat
50g net carbohydrates
2.3g fibre
9.9g protein

EQUIPMENT
Large ovenproof dish that will fit inside your slow cooker (optional).

INGREDIENTS
butter, for greasing
400ml full-fat milk
2 large eggs
grated zest of 2 oranges
8 slices of brioche
75g sultanas
75g dried cranberries
50g sugar

1 Ensure your slow cooker base or ovenproof dish is greased well with butter.

2 Beat the milk, eggs and orange zest in a bowl.

3 Layer the brioche in the dish or slow cooker base, sprinkle it with the sultanas, cranberries and sugar and pour over the milk and egg mixture. If using an ovenproof dish, cover with foil. If you are using an older style of slow cooker, place a trivet in the base of the cooker (see page 3) and place the dish on the trivet. Add boiling water until it reaches halfway up the sides of the dish. If you are cooking the pudding in your slow cooker base, you do not need to add boiling water.

4 Set to High, cover and cook for 2–3 hours.

5 Remove the pudding carefully from the slow cooker. If you like a crispy, browned top, place the pudding under a hot grill for 5–8 minutes until golden. If you are cooking the pudding in your slow cooker base, you do not need to add boiling water.

6 Serve with a dollop of cream, crème fraîche or Greek yogurt.

I love a good clafoutis but these flavours in particular are to die for! Serve with a dollop of extra-thick cream or ice cream for a really delicious dessert.

Raspberry and Pistachio Clafoutis

SERVES 8

NUTRITIONAL INFORMATION
PER SERVING
450 Kcals
34g fat
25g net carbohydrates
3.2g fibre
7.8g protein

INGREDIENTS
300ml double cream
25g butter, plus extra for
  greasing
1 tsp vanilla extract or paste
2 eggs, plus 3 egg yolks
120g sugar
50g ground almonds
70g plain flour, sifted
1 tsp baking powder
150g raspberries
2 tsp Chambord raspberry
  liqueur (optional)
75g unsalted shelled
  pistachios, roughly chopped

1 Preheat your slow cooker, following the manufacturer's instructions.

2 Grease the slow cooker pot really well with butter or use a cake liner or parchment to line it.

3 Heat the cream, butter and vanilla in a pan over a low heat until the butter has melted (do not allow it to boil). Remove from the heat and leave to cool.

4 Beat the eggs, egg yolks and sugar together in a bowl until light and fluffy. Add the ground almonds, flour and baking powder to the egg mixture and combine well, then gradually add the cream mixture to form a batter. Add the Chambord, if using. You can use a balloon whisk to ensure it is all mixed well.

5 Place the raspberries in the base of the slow cooker.

6 Pour the cake batter over the raspberries. Don't worry if the raspberries bob up. Scatter over the pistachios.

7 Cover your slow cooker with a tea towel before placing on the lid firmly, ensuring it is well secured.

8 Set to High and cook for 2–3 hours, until you have a light sponge that springs back when pressed.

9 Serve immediately with cream or ice cream.

Christmas

Chestnuts roasting on an open fire,

Jack Frost nipping at your nose . . . Yes, we all crave for an idyllic Christmas, but it can all get a bit stressful, hectic and exhausting and we need as many time-saving meals as possible.

Thankfully, the slow cooker is your friend at Christmas, and it is not just useful for cooking your Christmas pudding. There are many recipes that allow you to kick back, relax and let the slow cooker take the strain.

Remember to plan ahead and make use of your freezer. Making your own ready-meals and popping them in the freezer is an absolute godsend at this busy time of year. You will find notes on all the recipes in this book that are suitable for freezing.

The cranberries, brandy and spices give this dish a lovely Christmassy feel. It's ideal for a Christmas Eve winter-warmer that can be prepared in advance, leaving you more time to get on with your Christmas preparations. Serve it with steamed green vegetables and creamy mashed potatoes.

Beef and Cranberry Christmas Casserole

SERVES 4

NUTRITIONAL INFORMATION
PER SERVING
512 Kcals
9.2g fat
30g net carbohydrates
6.6g fibre
46g protein

INGREDIENTS
750g stewing beef, diced
1–2 tbsp plain flour
2 tsp paprika
2 tsp ground allspice
2 tsp olive or coconut oil
1 large red onion, finely
  chopped
2 garlic cloves, finely chopped
1 tsp ground ginger
½ tsp ground cinnamon
2 celery sticks, diced
1 large carrot, diced
1 sweet potato, peeled
  and diced
200g cranberries (fresh
  or frozen)
grated zest and juice of
  1 orange

100ml brandy
300ml red wine
1 beef stock cube (I use a
  beef stock pot)
salt and ground black pepper

1 If the diced beef isn't moist, wet it with a little water.

2 Mix the flour, paprika and allspice in a bowl, add the beef and toss to coat.

3 Preheat your slow cooker, following the manufacturer's instructions.

4 If your slow cooker has a sauté function, you can use this; if not, use a sauté pan on your hob. Heat the olive oil or coconut oil, add the onion and garlic and sauté for a couple of minutes, then add the beef and cook until brown. Place in the slow cooker (if you used a separate pan).

5 Add the remaining ingredients to the slow cooker, combine well and season with salt and pepper.

6 Set to Low, cover and cook for 6–8 hours.

7 Serve with green vegetables and mashed potatoes.

Christmas lunch can fill even the most experienced cook with dread, especially the turkey. If your slow cooker is big enough, you can simply cook a turkey crown in the slow cooker, which will guarantee super-moist meat. It won't colour, but you can pop it in the oven for 20 minutes to brown it at the end, if you wish.

Super-tender Turkey Crown

SERVES 8

NUTRITIONAL INFORMATION
PER SERVING
375 Kcals
10g fat
3.2g net carbohydrates
0.8g fibre
62g protein

INGREDIENTS
2 onions, roughly chopped
2 tsp rosemary
2 tsp thyme
2 bay leaves
2kg turkey crown (it must fit comfortably in your slow cooker)
75g butter
250ml white wine
250ml hot chicken stock
salt and ground black pepper

1 Preheat your slow cooker, following the manufacturer's instructions.

2 Place the onions and herbs in the base of your slow cooker.

3 Use an upturned dessertspoon to help lift the skin from the turkey crown to give you room to push the butter in. Use your hands to push the butter along the back of the crown and rub the butter under the skin directly onto the meat.

4 Place the turkey in the slow cooker. Pour over the wine and stock. Season with salt and pepper.

5 Set to High, cover and cook for 1 hour, then turn down to Low and cook for 6–8 hours (the cooking time will depend on the size of your turkey crown).

6 Remove the turkey from the slow cooker and cover it with foil. Leave it to rest for at least 30 minutes.

7 If you want to brown the turkey, preheat the oven to 210°C (190°C fan oven) Gas 7 then roast the turkey for 20–30 minutes until it has a nice golden colour. Avoid overcooking it in the oven or it will start to dry out.

8 Use the remaining stock and turkey juices in the slow cooker to make your gravy.

Christmas is not the same without a festive gammon. I like to roast mine after slow cooking it, as I believe it looks much nicer when presented with a crisp, golden layer of fat. I always buy a bigger joint than I need so I can have leftover ham to use in other recipes and for snacks.

Christmas Gammon

SERVES 8

NUTRITIONAL INFORMATION PER SERVING (BASED ON A 1KG GAMMON JOINT)
221 Kcals
9.4g fat
5.3g net carbohydrates
0.8g fibre
22g protein

INGREDIENTS
1 gammon joint (about 1kg)
750ml dry cider
2 bay leaves
2 tsp ground allspice
2 cinnamon sticks
2–3cm piece of fresh ginger, peeled and roughly chopped
1 orange, quartered
salt and ground black pepper
c. 50 cloves

1 Preheat your slow cooker, following the manufacturer's instructions.

2 Place the gammon in the slow cooker.

3 Pour in the cider. Add the bay leaves, a few of the cloves, allspice, cinnamon sticks, ginger and orange quarters. Season with pepper.

4 Set to Low, cover and cook for 6–8 hours, or set to High and cook for 4–5 hours.

5 You can roast the gammon after slow cooking if you want to crisp up the fat on the outside. Preheat the oven to 210°C (190°C fan oven) Gas 7. Remove the gammon from the slow cooker and score the fat with a sharp knife to form diamond shapes. Stud the gammon with the remaining cloves. Place in a roasting tray and roast for 30 minutes, until golden.

6 Remove from the oven and allow to rest before slicing.

You can't have Christmas lunch without this spicy red cabbage. It is so yummy and goes well with turkey. You can double up the recipe and store the cabbage in sterilised jars in the fridge for up to a week, to serve as a pickle at a later date.

Festive Spiced Red Cabbage

MAKES ABOUT 750G

NUTRITIONAL INFORMATION
PER 100G
31 Kcals
0.3g fat
5.5g net carbohydrates
0.8g protein

INGREDIENTS
1 red cabbage, finely shredded
1 large apple, peeled, cored
  and diced
2 red onions, finely chopped
grated zest and juice of
  1 orange
2 tsp ground allspice
150ml red wine vinegar or port
salt and ground black pepper

1 Preheat your slow cooker, following the manufacturer's instructions.

2 Place all the ingredients in the slow cooker and stir to combine. Season to taste.

3 Set to Low, cover and cook for 5–6 hours.

4 Serve hot or cold.

Get into the Christmas spirit and make this amazing sauce – the whole house will smell wonderfully Christmassy afterwards. This recipe is rich and boozy. If you prefer not to use the alcohol, you can replace the port and brandy with water. The sauce can be kept in the fridge for up to a week and it also freezes well.

Cranberry Sauce

MAKES ABOUT 700G
VG

NUTRITIONAL INFORMATION
PER 100G
31 Kcals
0.2g fat
5.1g net carbohydrates
0.4g protein

INGREDIENTS
500g cranberries
  (fresh or frozen)
1 cooking apple, peeled,
  cored and diced
150ml port
75ml brandy
grated zest and juice of
  2 oranges
½ tsp ground allspice
150g sugar (or to taste)
2 cinnamon sticks

1 Preheat your slow cooker, following the manufacturer's instructions.

2 Place all ingredients in the slow cooker and stir well to ensure everything is well mixed.

3 Set to High, cover and cook for 1½–2 hours, stirring occasionally.

4 Remove the cinnamon sticks. Place in a serving dish, or store in sterilised jars until ready to use.

This is a lighter alternative to the traditional Christmas pudding. I like to flavour the sponge with orange as I feel it is a nice contrast to the mincemeat, but if you love the Christmassy flavours, you could omit the orange zest and add some mixed spice and cinnamon instead. This recipe is also delicious with some dried cranberries added to the sponge mixture. Serve it warm with homemade custard, ice cream or crème fraîche.

Orange and Mincemeat Sponge Pudding

SERVES 6–8

NUTRITIONAL
INFORMATION PER SERVING
(FOR 8 SERVINGS)
465 Kcals
22g fat
60g net carbohydrates
1.9g fibre
6g protein

EQUIPMENT
You will need a 1.2-litre pudding bowl, baking parchment, foil and string (I like to use double-sided foil from Lakeland, with foil on one side and parchment on the other).

INGREDIENTS
3–4 tbsp mincemeat
175g butter, softened, plus
  extra for greasing
175g sugar
3 large eggs
225g self-raising flour
grated zest of 2–3 oranges

1 Grease the pudding bowl thoroughly and generously with butter and set to one side.

2 Spoon the mincemeat into the base of the pudding bowl.

3 Cream the butter and sugar together in a bowl until light and fluffy. Add the eggs, beat well, then sift the flour into the bowl and fold it in gently. Fold in the orange zest.

4 Place the mixture into your pudding bowl. Cover the pudding bowl with baking parchment, pleating it at the centre to allow for expansion, then add a pleated layer of foil and tie very securely with string. Make a handle with string or foil to make it easier to lift the pudding in and out of the slow cooker (see page 153).

5 Boil the kettle. Place the pudding in the base of your slow cooker. If you are using an older style of slow cooker, place a trivet into the base of the cooker (see page 3). Add boiling water to the slow cooker until it comes halfway up the sides of the pudding bowl.

6 Set to High, cover and cook for 3–4 hours, or set to Low, cover and cook for 6–8 hours, or until the sponge springs back when touched.

7 Remove the pudding from the slow cooker using the handle. Run a knife around the edge of the pudding. Place a plate on the top of the bowl and carefully flip the plate and bowl, to turn out the pudding.

8 Serve warm with custard, ice cream or crème fraîche.

It's not Christmas without a Christmas pudding. This is one of my favourites and it is pretty foolproof, even when made at the last minute. Remember, Christmas pudding darkens as it cooks, so don't worry if you think it looks pale when you are making it.

Christmas Pudding

SERVES 8

NUTRITIONAL INFORMATION
PER SERVING
412 Kcals
12g fat
63g net carbohydrates
4.7g fibre
5.8g protein

EQUIPMENT
You will need a 1.2-litre
pudding bowl, baking
parchment, foil and string
(I like to use double-sided foil
from Lakeland, with foil on
one side and parchment on
the other).

INGREDIENTS
butter or lard, for greasing
80g plain flour
2 tsp mixed spice
2 tsp ground allspice
2 tsp ground cinnamon
75g suet (you can use beef
  or vegetarian)
150g dark brown sugar
30g dried apricots, diced
→

1 Grease the pudding bowl thoroughly and generously with butter or lard and set to one side. You can place a circle of baking parchment in the base of the bowl if you are worried about the pudding sticking.

2 Sift the flour and spices together into a bowl.

3 Add the suet, brown sugar, dried fruit, almonds, breadcrumbs and mixed peel and mix well.

4 Add the grated apple, orange zest and juice, eggs and brandy and stir well until all ingredients are well combined.

5 Place the mixture into your pudding bowl. Cover the pudding bowl with baking parchment, pleating it at the centre to allow for expansion, then add a pleated layer of foil and tie very securely with string. Make a handle with string or foil to make it easier to lift the pudding in and out of the slow cooker (see page 153).

6 Boil the kettle. Place the pudding in the base of your slow cooker. If you are using an older style of slow cooker, place a trivet into the base of the cooker (see page 3). Add boiling water to the slow cooker until it comes halfway up the sides of the pudding bowl.

7 Set to Low, cover and cook for 8 hours; the longer the cook, the darker the pudding.

8 Remove the pudding from the slow cooker using the handle.

140g currants
135g raisins
135g sultanas
30g almonds, roughly chopped
60g fresh white breadcrumbs
50g mixed peel
1 cooking apple, grated
  (no need to peel)
grated zest and juice of
  1 orange
2 eggs, beaten
60ml brandy

9 To reheat the pudding, set it in your slow cooker with boiling water as detailed in step 6, set to High, cover and cook for 3 hours.

10 When ready to serve, remove the parchment and run a knife around the edge of the pudding. Place a plate on the top of the bowl and carefully flip the plate and bowl, to turn out the pudding.

TOP TIP
The pudding can be made a few months before Christmas and stored in a cool, dark place. Feed it occasionally with brandy.

Your slow cooker is perfect for making delicious mulled wine. It has the advantage of keeping the wine warm while you entertain without a worry. You can buy sachets of aromatics for your mulled wine but I prefer to create my own blend. I also like to add a little brandy, but this is entirely optional. I don't sweeten my mulled wine, but if you like it sweet, you could add a tablespoon or two of honey to taste.

Mulled Wine

SERVES 8

NUTRITIONAL INFORMATION
PER 175ML SERVING
188 Kcals
0g fat
9.7g net carbohydrates
0g fibre
0.5g protein

INGREDIENTS
750ml bottle red wine
250ml brandy (optional)
2 oranges, thickly sliced
3 cloves
2–3 cinnamon sticks
2 star anise
3–4 tbsp honey (optional)

1 Preheat your slow cooker, following the manufacturer's instructions.

2 Place all the ingredients in the slow cooker.

3 Set to High, cover and cook for 45 minutes.

4 Switch to Warm when ready to serve.

5 Serve the mulled wine in heatproof glasses.

Pantry

Your slow cooker is so versatile:

it can make broths, sauces, preserves and more. If you want to make preserves or chutneys, please read the tips over the page to ensure your jars are correctly sterilised and stored.

Sterilise!

Before you start cooking preserves or chutneys, you need to sterilise your jars. You can do this in your dishwasher or use this more traditional technique:

1 Preheat the oven to 120°C (100°C fan oven) Gas ¼.

2 Wash the jars and their lids thoroughly in warm, clean, soapy water, rinse and place upside down on a clean tea towel to drain. Place the jars (and their lids, if the lids are ovenproof) on a baking tray or directly onto the oven rack.

3 Place in the preheated oven for 15 minutes, then turn the oven to its lowest setting to keep the jars warm while you make the preserve/chutney. When removing the jars from the oven, place them on an old newspaper or clean tea towel. If the jars were directly on the oven rack, take care not to burn yourself when you remove them. Be careful not to touch the inside of the jars as you may contaminate them.

Storage

All the sauces in this chapter can be frozen or stored in an airtight container in the fridge for up to 1 week. Chutneys can be stored for up to 3 months if kept in sterilised jars. Curds stored in sterilised jars in the fridge will keep for up to 3 months if unopened, or 6 weeks in a cool, dark place, and up to 1 week once opened. I tend to keep curds in small jars to avoid wastage. Stocks can be kept in the fridge for up to four days, or can be frozen.

This healthy broth is much better for you than processed stock cubes. It is packed with minerals such as calcium, magnesium and phosphorus, as well as collagen, glucosamine and hyaluronic acid and a wide range of vitamins. It helps support the digestive tract, boosts the immune system, reduces inflammation, strengthens joints, hair and nails and promotes healthy skin. Your butcher may be happy to give away bones for you to use.

Bone Broth

INGREDIENTS

1kg meaty bones (marrow bone, marrow, ribs, knuckles etc.)
200ml apple cider vinegar
2 large onions, quartered
2 garlic cloves, cut into chunks
2 carrots, cut into chunks
2–3 celery sticks, cut into chunks
2 tsp mixed herbs
2–3 tsp parsley
2–3 bay leaves
2 tsp black peppercorns

1 Preheat your slow cooker, following the manufacturer's instructions.

2 Place all the ingredients in your slow cooker and cover with water.

3 Set to Low, cover and cook for 24–48 hours.

4 You may want to skim any scum from the surface of the water occasionally using a slotted spoon.

5 Remove the bones and strain the broth. Leave to cool overnight or for at least 3–4 hours. A layer of fat will form on the top once cooled and settled. Remove the fat, leaving a clear stock.

6 Store the stock in jars, freezer bags or in silicone ice cube moulds, ready to use in your everyday savoury dishes. Store in the fridge for up to 4 days or freeze for up to 3 months.

TOP TIP

I store my broth in freezer bags and in large silicone ice cube moulds. The freezer bags can be defrosted quickly by popping the sealed bag into a bowl of warm water. I use the silicone moulds to pop out a few small 'ice' stocks to add to dishes such as a chilli or spaghetti bolognese during cooking.

The recipe is similar in principle to the bone broth on page 199, but chicken bones do not need to cook for as long as beef bones. You can use roasted chicken carcasses for this, which saves throwing them away! Chicken wings, once roasted, also make a delicious stock. In fact, you can use any poultry carcass, including turkey, guinea fowl and duck.

Chicken Broth

INGREDIENTS

1 cooked chicken carcass or
  chicken bones
1 large onion, quartered
1 carrot, cut into chunks
2–3 celery sticks, cut into
  chunks
2 tsp thyme
a small handful of fresh
  parsley (or 2–3 tsp dried
  parsley)
2–3 bay leaves
2 tsp black peppercorns

1 Preheat your slow cooker, following the manufacturer's instructions.

2 Place all the ingredients in your slow cooker and cover with water.

3 Set to Low, cover and cook for 8–12 hours.

4 When cooked, strain the broth. Leave to cool.

5 Store the stock in jars, freezer bags or in silicone ice cube moulds ready to use in your everyday savoury dishes. Store in the fridge for up to 4 days or freeze for up to 3 months.

There really is no fixed recipe for vegetable stock; anything goes. I normally raid my vegetable drawer and pull out anything that is no longer suitable for fresh vegetable dishes. I also include the bits of veg we would normally throw away, such as broccoli stalks and onion skins, as they still have lots of flavour.

Vegetable Stock

1 Preheat your slow cooker, following the manufacturer's instructions.

2 Place your chosen ingredients in your slow cooker and cover with water. Add any chosen herbs and seasoning – such as mixed herbs, parsley, thyme or oregano. Season with salt and pepper.

3 Set to Low, cover and cook for 8 hours.

4 When cooked, strain the stock. Leave to cool.

5 Store the stock in jars, freezer bags or in silicone ice cube moulds ready to use in your everyday savoury dishes. Store in the fridge for up to 4 days or freeze for up to 3 months.

This is a huge favourite of mine. It's delicious served with cheese and crackers, or why not use it as a base for a red onion and goat's cheese tart?

Red Onion Chutney

MAKES AROUND 1KG

NUTRITIONAL INFORMATION
PER 20G SERVING
26 Kcals
0.5g fat
4.3g net carbohydrates
0g fibre
0g protein

INGREDIENTS
30g butter
8 red onions, thinly sliced
120g dark brown sugar
75g sultanas
2 tsp paprika
150ml red wine
50ml balsamic vinegar
salt and ground black pepper

1 Preheat your slow cooker, following the manufacturer's instructions.

2 If your slow cooker has a sauté function, you can use this; if not, use a frying pan or sauté pan on the hob. Heat the butter, add the onions and cook until the onions are soft and translucent. Place in the slow cooker (if you used a separate pan).

3 Add all the remaining ingredients and season with salt and pepper.

4 Set to Low, cover and cook for 6 hours until thick and caramelised – you should not need to add any more liquid, but if it looks too dry, add a dash more wine.

5 Store in sterilised jars in the fridge.

This is a sweet and slightly spicy chutney that complements meat and rice dishes well, but is also delicious simply served with bread and cheese.

Plum and Apple Chutney

MAKES ABOUT 2KG

VG

NUTRITIONAL INFORMATION
PER 30G SERVING

35 Kcals
0g fat
7.7g net carbohydrates
0g fibre
0g protein

INGREDIENTS

600g red onions, diced
1kg Bramley apples, peeled,
  cored and diced
400g plums, stoned and diced
150g sultanas
30g fresh ginger, peeled and
  finely chopped
3 star anise
2 tsp ground cinnamon
2 tsp ground cumin
1–3 red or green chillies, finely
  chopped (depending on your
  personal taste)
400g sugar
350ml apple cider vinegar

1 Preheat your slow cooker, following the manufacturer's instructions.

2 Place all the ingredients in the slow cooker and stir well until evenly combined.

3 Set to Low, cover and cook for 6 hours.

4 If you want to thicken it, simmer it on High for 30 minutes. If you want to thin the mixture, add a little water.

5 When you have achieved the right consistency, store it into sterilised jars in the fridge.

Traditionally, Seville oranges are used to make marmalade. The small, very sour oranges are in season at the beginning of the year. You can use regular sweet oranges if you prefer, but may want to reduce the amount of sugar. I have added Cointreau to this marmalade because it's delicious, but you can make it with brandy, whisky or leave out the alcohol if you prefer!

Seville Orange and Cointreau Marmalade

FILLS ABOUT 6 STANDARD-SIZE JAM JARS

NUTRITIONAL INFORMATION PER 20G SERVING
31 Kcals
0g fat
7.3g net carbohydrates
0g fibre
0g protein

EQUIPMENT
You will need a muslin bag and 6 sterilised jam jars.

INGREDIENTS
1kg Seville oranges
  (or ordinary oranges)
2 large lemons
1.5kg granulated or preserving
  sugar
150ml Cointreau (optional)

1 Wash the fruit to get rid of any dirt or wax coating.

2 Quarter the oranges and lemons and remove all the pith and the pips. Make sure you do this over a bowl or tray to retain all the juice. All of the fruit is used when making marmalade – the peel, pith and pips help to give the marmalade a good set.

3 Place the pith and pips into a muslin bag and tie tightly.

4 Pour any juice into the slow cooker and add 1.5 litres of water.

5 Slice the peel into strips on a chopping board with a sharp knife – cut it thickly or thinly, depending on your personal preference.

6 Place the strips of peel in the cooker and lay the muslin bag on the top.

7 Set to Low, cover and cook for 10–12 hours (you can leave it to cook overnight).

8 The next day, pour the mixture into a large saucepan, or a preserving pan if you have one (discarding the muslin bag) and heat the mixture until it is simmering. Add the sugar and Cointreau (if using), and stir over a medium-high until the sugar has dissolved.

9 Bring to the boil and boil rapidly for 10–15 minutes.

10 Test the marmalade for setting point by putting a teaspoon of the mixture onto a cold plate. After 10 minutes, gently push the liquid with your index finger. If the surface wrinkles with small creases, it is ready to put into jars. If not, boil for a little longer and repeat the setting test. Marmalade can take longer to set than other jams.

11 When the marmalade reaches setting point, pour it into sterilised jars.

I love lemon curd. I use it to sandwich layers of lemon sponge, along with buttercream. I also add a dollop to the centre of lemon cupcakes and sometimes have it for breakfast with Greek yogurt, nuts and berries. My son loves it on toast so, all in all, it is a vital ingredient in the Flower household.

Lemon Curd

FILLS ABOUT 2 STANDARD-SIZED JAM JARS

NUTRITIONAL INFORMATION PER 20G SERVING
39 Kcals
2g fat
4.2g net carbohydrates
0g fibre
0.7g protein

EQUIPMENT
You will need a 1.2 litre pudding bowl, foil and 2 sterilised jam jars.

INGREDIENTS
100g butter
200g caster sugar
grated zest and juice of 4 large lemons (removing any pips)
4 eggs

1 Place the butter, sugar, lemon zest and juice in your pudding bowl. Place the bowl in the slow cooker and pour boiling water around the bowl until it comes halfway up the sides of the bowl. Set to Low, cover and cook for 20 minutes.

2 Remove the bowl from the slow cooker and leave to cool for 5 minutes. Keep the slow cooker on as you will be returning the bowl to the cooker.

3 Beat the eggs. Quickly pour them into the lemon mixture while beating constantly with a balloon whisk to ensure the eggs don't curdle.

4 Place a large sheet of foil over the bowl and crimp it around the edges of the bowl to secure.

5 Place the bowl back into the slow cooker, keeping the temperature set to Low. Add more boiling water around the bowl, ensuring the water comes just over halfway up the sides of the bowl.

6 Cover and cook for 2–3 hours, removing the bowl and foil lid and stirring the curd a couple of times to avoid any lumps. If you forget to stir and it goes lumpy or curdles, whisk it well with a balloon whisk and it will come good.

7 The curd should be thick enough to hold when poured from the back of a spoon, but not too thick and lumpy.

8 When ready, pour the curd into sterilised jars. Cover the surface of the curd with a circle of parchment before sealing with lids. Keep refrigerated once opened.

A few years ago, I gave my parents a rather posh Christmas hamper. Inside it were some lovely jars of preserved fruits that they raved about. I came up with this simple slow-cooker recipe for boozy apricots to recreate those amazing flavours. I have used fresh apricots and cognac, but you can choose any fruit and alcohol to suit your taste. I would suggest trying pears, peaches or plums, topped with brandy, rum, vodka, amaretto or kirsch.

Boozy Preserved Apricots

MAKES 1 LARGE JAR
(6–8 SERVINGS)

NUTRITIONAL
INFORMATION PER SERVING
(FOR 8 SERVINGS)
285 Kcals
0g fat
53g net carbohydrates
0.8g fibre
0g protein

INGREDIENTS
8 fresh apricots, halved and
  stones removed
200g sugar
200–300ml cognac

1 Place the apricot halves in the slow cooker, add the sugar and 300ml water and stir until combined.

2 Set to High, cover and cook for 1–1½ hours to help soften the fruit.

3 Turn off and leave to cool.

4 Place the apricots into your sterilised jar. Add 2–3 tablespoons of the remaining fruit syrup to the jar. Top with the cognac until the fruit is completely covered. Seal and shake a few times to ensure the syrup and alcohol is mixed. Store in the fridge until needed. They should keep up to 3 months before the alcohol starts to break down the fruit.

TOP TIP
The harder the fruit, the more they need softening. You can use cherries or figs and these can be placed straight in the jar with the sugar and alcohol as they do not need to be softened.

Index